WOMAN
ACCEPTABLE EXPLOITATION FOR PROFIT

SHREELA FLATHER

Whittles Publishing

Published by
Whittles Publishing,
Dunbeath,
Caithness KW6 6EY,
Scotland, UK

www.whittlespublishing.com

© 2010 S Flather

ISBN 978-184995-002-2

Printed and bound in the UK by J F Print Ltd., Sparkford, Somerset

CONTENTS

Introduction   v
The World in Which We Live   vii

1   WHY WE NEED TO CHANGE   1
2   AFRICAN WOMAN   11
3   INDIAN WOMAN   23
4   THE BLAME GAME   34
5   WOMEN VERSUS WOMEN AND OTHER
      FORMS OF VIOLENCE   50
6   THE MILLENNIUM DEVELOPMENT GOALS   60
7   CHILD LABOUR – THE GREAT TABOO   75
8   GLOBALISATION – PART OF THE SOLUTION   81
9   THE OPPOSITION   89
10 FIRST STEPS   99
11 RISKS AND REWARDS   116

Postscript   125
Examples to Inspire Action   131

INTRODUCTION

My proposition is based on sex and profits. This is not a book about Women's Lib, but it is a book which will lead to the recognition of women carried along by the wholehearted support of men; it is not another call for charitable donations, but it is a book about investment.

The poorest women of the Indian sub-continent and Africa represent a vast untapped resource and are easy to find. They are hard-working and eager to learn – the perfect workforce. But today they have no sense of self-worth; they murder their own baby daughters because they are deemed to be of no value, indeed harbingers of debt; too often they are regarded as little more than beasts of burden, or they are hidden away, deprived of education and position.

I want to turn these countless millions of wives, mothers and daughters into profit generators for themselves and for the global business community. I will tread on a few toes along the way, tackle the great taboo of children working for a living and face up to arguments against managing an ever-increasing population using birth control. You can't talk about the role of women in isolation from their sex lives.

I will challenge politicians to turn talking shops into practical action; the much vaunted United Nations Millennium Development Goals (MDGs) dream cannot be fulfilled by the target date of 2015. Its only hope is to shift the focus to women. While the UN rightly identifies the private sector as the 'engine of innovation and growth', it fails by not targeting that effort at women directly. As part and parcel of that refocusing, it should start talking about family planning.

Women must be central to every initiative, business project and political goal, rather than afterthoughts or decoration. And, dare I say, this is just as applicable to the West, and the UK in particular, where the Equality and Human Rights Commission reported in September 2008 that the number of women in top jobs was actually falling; far from breaking through the glass ceiling, women have crashed into impenetrable triple-glazing. So let no one say that the case for women's rights anywhere in the world has been addressed fully, let alone met. When we stop saying with surprise that the head of some corporation or organisation is a woman, then I will feel satisfied. I am convinced that if the male mindset can be changed then the women will take care of the rest. The result will be profit for business, income and welfare for poor families, rescue for the environment and votes for politicians.

The arrogance is not in maintaining that any single idea can bring about a change: rather it is in believing that the status quo can continue. As we slide ever deeper into global economic depression, this above all is a hopeful book offering a practical, affordable way forward. It requires no new energy source, it demands no vast capital investment and it will have no destructive impact on the environment. The workforce is vast, willing and able. A mother will not squander her money; she will nourish her children rather than drinking herself into oblivion, and she will remain loyal to her family.

This is not about charity. It is not about improving the education of women. It is all about income generation.

Woman: Acceptable Exploitation for Profit is a solution for a world in trouble, a roadmap to greater opportunities, profit, prosperity, health and happiness for all, regardless of gender. And before this notion is dismissed as fanciful wishful thinking, critics should first consider some of the examples (see page 131) where a handful of enlightened business leaders are already reaping the rewards, just as their new female workforce are transforming their own lives and those of their families and villages. This is not pie-in-the-sky: it is happening, but so far this practical and demonstrably successful concept has not received the recognition it deserves. We live in a world struggling to feed itself, fund itself, preserve itself, so why reject an asset and talent we have failed to consider?

THE WORLD IN WHICH WE LIVE

- There are 6.7 billion people in the world – there will be another 2.6 billion by 2050 (US Bureau of the Census).

- While Europe is anticipating a 14 per cent fall in its overall population by 2050, Africa is likely to witness an increase of 130 per cent (UN Population Division).

- One woman dies every minute from pregnancy-related issues – 41 per cent of pregnancies globally are unwanted (Department of International Development – UK Government).

- There is a direct correlation between high fertility and high child mortality rates (UN Economic Commission for Africa).

- 'If you save mothers, you improve the chances of children' (Sarah Brown, wife of the British Prime Minister, Gordon Brown).

- 'The ability of women to control their own fertility is absolutely fundamental to women's empowerment and equality' (United Nations Population Fund – UNFPA).

- Between 2002 and 2008, the Bush administration withheld a total of US$235 million authorised by Congress to the UNFPA, the United Nations Population Fund, which supports family planning and reproductive health care programmes in 154 countries (UK All Party Parliamentary Group on Population Development and Reproductive Health).

- Nine million children die every year from malnutrition before they are five years old, having suffered a life of hunger and misery (World Health Organization).

- There are 250 million child labourers worldwide aged between 5 and 14 (International Labour Organization).

- India has more malnourished people than any other country in the world – 200 million are hungry (Global Hunger Index, 2008).

- In monetary terms, three quarters of India's 1.2 billion people live on 30p a day.

- 40 per cent of Africans go to bed hungry every night (UNICEF).

- An African child dies every six seconds from disease or extreme poverty (UNICEF).

- 43 per cent of children in sub-Saharan Africa do not have safe, accessible drinking water (UNICEF).

- Two thirds of the world's population will face moderate to high water shortages by 2025 (United Nations).

- Children account for half of all civilian casualties in wars in Africa (AFRICA, 2015).

- At least 28 wars have been fought in sub-Saharan Africa since the 1970s.

- In November 2008 it was reported that 1,500 people were dying in the conflict in the Democratic Republic of Congo every day (International Rescue Committee).

- Between 1996 and 2006, as many as ten million female foetuses – 1 in 25 – were aborted in India (*The Lancet*).

- 'Women are not dying because of diseases we cannot treat … they are dying because societies have yet to make the decision that their lives are worth saving' (Dr Mahmoud Fathalla, Professor of Obstetrics and Gynaecology at Assiut University in Egypt and a former Director of the WHO Special Programme of Research, Development and Research Training in Human Reproduction, 2003).

- One woman in five around the world is likely to be the victim of rape or attempted rape in her lifetime (World Health Organization).

- Somewhere in America, a woman is raped every two minutes (US Department of Justice). It is estimated that only 37 per cent of cases get reported (FBI).

- Between 20 per cent and 50 per cent of women in every country suffer domestic violence. (UNICEF, *Domestic Violence Against Women and Girls*).

- Domestic violence causes more death and disability among women aged 15–45 years than cancer, malaria, traffic accidents and war (Human Rights Watch, *World Report*, 2000).

- It is estimated that violence against women in the UK costs society £40 billion each year (New Philanthropy Capital).

- 100 million to 140 million girls and women worldwide are living with the consequences of female genital mutilation (World Health Organization).

- One person is infected with HIV every six seconds – so the total number of infections is growing (UNFPA).

- Of the estimated 39.5 million people living with HIV, 70 per cent are women and half of all new infections occur among women (Population Resource Center, World Aids Day, 1 December 2006).

- Female trafficking – 100,000 women were sold in 2002 (United Nations).

- By 2008 the UK's Home Office had investigated some 500 cases of alleged forced marriage.

- 189 countries signed up to the Millennium Development Goals at the United Nations Millennium Summit in 2000 – all now accept that they cannot be achieved.

8 July 2005 – Gleneagles, Scotland

Rock stars Bob Geldof and Bono praised the world leaders at the G8 summit for pledging to double aid to Africa to $50 billion. They said it would save the lives of hundreds of thousands of people who would have died of poverty, malaria or Aids.

18 June 2008 – Paris, France

Geldof and Bono condemned the 'miserable' failure of rich nations to fulfill pledges made on African aid. According to a report by advocacy group Data, published by the two stars, the G8 had only delivered 14 per cent of what was promised.

1

WHY WE NEED TO CHANGE

It is pretty clear that we cannot rely on politicians to make a difference to the wretched lives of the millions living in poverty in Africa and Asia, so we had better search elsewhere.

When we consider the state of the world we may feel that, with all our modern conveniences, life is getting better, give or take a few economic upsets. They will always happen: for every boom there will be a correction, if not always a bust. When we were told the world was looking into an economic abyss in 2009 because of bank failures, commentators were forgetting history. There have been only two years since 1934 when no US bank failed (2005 and 2006), and 1,000 closed during 1988 and 1989,[1] yet somehow we survived. Yes, the financial sector in the UK generates a large share of our Gross Domestic Product, but it only employs 10 per cent of the

---

1   Mark Perry, Professor of Economics at the University of Michigan.

workforce so I suspect we will pull through. Profits rise and fall, businesses rise and fall – that is the harsh law of economics. But for millions living in abject poverty in Africa and India the times of boom pass them by. They never had anything, and unless someone speaks up for them they never will. This is not a case of let's be nice to the poor for a change. What is happening on these continents will have an impact on us all. We profess great concern for the environment, but we seem slow to admit that population and environment are inextricably linked. Environment is population, economy is population, social collapse is population, and population is women because men have never taken responsibility for family planning. There are 6.7 billion of us already, with another 2 billion plus predicted by 2050, and we have all got to be fed and watered – that's the simple link. All humanity is connected.

If we cannot be persuaded to help those less fortunate than ourselves out of charity and aid, and it is perfectly plain from the Geldof and Bono comments that we are not, then at least we might think of helping them because it could lead to greater profits.

But before we deal with the solution, let me explain the problem in outline. I explore the facts in more detail later – it doesn't make pleasant reading. First, let's look at Africa, where there seems to be an inability to manage growth and development as easily as politicians amass wealth and power. There is talk of debt reduction, commissions on the future of Africa and so many major initiatives, but where does the money actually go? Who has it helped? The money does not reach the people for whom it was intended, that's for sure. So while 14 per cent of the $59 billion was said to have been pledged, I doubt whether even a tiny fraction of that aid reached the poorest in the remote rural villages.

What is life really like in Africa and the Indian sub-continent, particularly for the women? In short, it is horrifying. Quite apart from the crimes perpetrated against women – rape, beatings and all other forms of abuse by their attackers – there is also the brutality of the culture meted out by those closest to them. Female genital mutilation is widespread as is inadequate (or no) access to obstetric or gynaecological care. In northern Nigeria, for example, a hundred thousand women are suffering from fistula because they were sold as wives as soon as they reached puberty, became pregnant immediately and gave birth. There is nobody there to help them with the childbirth, and labour can last for four or five days – in itself unimaginable in a western country. Invariably, that baby is stillborn and the mother's internal organs are split. Without treatment, which would be 90 per cent successful in the West, they are condemned to the pain and humiliation of incontinence. It is estimated that 300 million women in developing countries have illnesses stemming from pregnancy and childbirth.[2] The figures may well be worse, as facts are difficult to find in the culture of silence compounded by stigma and shame.[3] The concept of post-natal depression is commonly rejected,[4] and yet the evidence suggests that maternal mental health is a critical and largely ignored factor in the ability of a newborn child to thrive, particularly in low-income countries.[5]

What do the men do? They throw their wives out on the streets and find another one. Women are totally replaceable. If they get too old, their husbands just take another. The terrible irony is that men never seem to think that *they* are too old. At the end of 2008, Britain's Channel Four TV ran a gruesomely graphic documentary about child brides in northern Nigeria. Despite the central government passing the Child's Rights Act in 2003, forbidding marriage before a girl is 18 years old, it seems that every state is allowed to interpret the law according to its own customs and traditions. Only one state in northern Nigeria adopted the act, and then it replaced '18 years' with 'puberty'. Nearly half of all girls are married by the age of 15, usually to older men. The documentary showed a grizzled old man in his eighties grinning with delight as he explained that he had recently married a child of around 12 because, apparently, he needed a fertile wife. There then followed in harrowing detail the effects of fistula – one young woman had suffered from it twice and lost six babies. The reporter interviewed a group of men squatting under a tree, and about half knew of wives dying in childbirth. One imam sitting in front of his copy of the Qur'an said that there was nothing in the holy book to prevent a man even marrying a child of one year, provided the marriage was not consummated before she was physically or psychologically able. The argument seemed to be that it was in the girl's own best interest, as she then avoided the temptation of pre-marital sex.[6]

Don't look for leadership from the top in the matter of multiple brides. Some kings and heads of state set such bad examples, taking several wives at the same time in some macabre *droit de seigneur* – King Mswati III of Swaziland, the last remaining absolute monarch in the world, had 14 wives by the time he was 40 years old. His father had 70 when he died.

Thirty per cent of women in the caring sector are believed to be HIV positive because they get raped. In South Africa rape is endemic. If you look at sub-Saharan Africa, women are raped not only by strangers but by members of the family, even

---

2 WHO, 2005.

3 Zurayk, H., Khattab, H., Younis, N., El-Mouelhy, M., and Fadle, M. Concepts and measures of reproductive morbidity, *Health Transition Review*, 3(1), 17–40, 1993.

4 UK All Party Parliamentary Group on Population, Development and Reproductive Health, October 2008.

5 Patel, V. and Kirkwood, B. Treating maternal depression with community health workers. *The Lancet*, 372, 868–9, 2008; Prince, M., Patel, V., Saxena, S., *et al*. No health without mental health. *The Lancet*, 370, 859–77, 2007.

6 Channel Four News – Unreported World. *Nigeria: Child Brides Stolen Lives* by Ramita Navai, 2008.

church leaders and teachers, people in positions of trust. In that kind of situation, effectively half the population is being treated as sub-human by the other half. But you can't have 50 per cent of the population regarded as inferior while the other 50 per cent think only about themselves and still expect daily life in their countries to improve. How can we change the mindset of a place like Pakistan, where there are communities such as the Qambrani Baloch, where it is tradition to marry off – sell, I would call it – their daughters upon reaching puberty, who might be as young as 12? Girls are discouraged from going to school and seeking employment.

Is there going to be some miracle? I don't think so. I don't believe in miracles. It will need something drastic and original to make a difference – something that has never been tried, and to me it is quite obvious that the one untapped resource is precisely these poor women. They have had nothing since the day they were born; even in childhood, as girls, they would be expected to look after the boys who, from an early age, seem to be trained not to do anything. In that situation, the only untried resource is woman – someone with infinite skills, fortitude and patience, in short a caring workforce that doesn't drink, or fight, or gamble.

By contrast, when we look at India we have an incredible picture. Business was booming until 2008, with Indian companies buying up the great names of the western world, companies that have almost come to symbolise the West, like Jaguar the car manufacturer. There is a great deal of focus on India. Isn't it amazing how well she is doing? Indeed, it is. Indians have always been clever, natural entrepreneurs, and it is wonderful to see how the country is progressing.

But while the rich are getting so rich that it would make Croesus blush, what is happening to the rest of the country? There is a middle level, if not exactly middle class, who are benefiting from the boom times: the milkman who might once have come on foot now arrives on a scooter; even servants to the wealthy are getting bigger perks. But as you might expect, the poorest of the poor in the outlying rural communities are getting even poorer. According to the Global Hunger Index 2008,[7] India has more malnourished people than any other country in the world – 200 million are hungry. It reported: 'Despite years of robust economic growth, India scored worse than nearly 25 sub-Saharan African countries and all of South Asia, except Bangladesh.' This is in a country that is self-sufficient in food grains and yet, in monetary terms, three quarters of the nation's 1.2 billion people live on 30p a day.

Every year the government sets aside billions of pounds for poverty alleviation. But how much actually reaches the poor? I was at a conference recently and suggested

---

7   The Global Hunger Index was produced by the International Food Policy Research Institute (IFPRI) in collaboration with Germany's Welthungerhilfe and Concern Worldwide and released on World Hunger Day (16 October 2008).

that perhaps only 10 per cent trickled all the way down. I was quickly corrected and told that it was more like 5 per cent. This is the depressing picture of India today where, if you talk about poverty, the poorest of the poor are always the women, because whatever resources are available go to the men. It is the unspoken rule that boy is king and man is emperor. The women eat last, having fed first the husbands, then the children, and often there is not much left for them. The girl child may also be malnourished as she too comes second.

There is plenty of evidence about the neglect of girls. The curse of the dowry hangs over women, and it really is a curse. When a girl is born, she is immediately regarded as a burden of debt on the family. A boy is an asset. The girl will not bring anything into the family: quite the contrary, her parents will have to pay a boy to marry her in the form of the dowry; it may be outlawed today, but it is still normal practice. It is an appalling concept to have to buy a man for your daughter. After marriage, life is no better as she becomes a virtual slave without rights or say in any decision. Little wonder, then, that we hear about the appalling practice of female foetus killings, the abortion of perfectly healthy female babies. Just like the dowry, it is outlawed; just like the dowry, it is still practised, especially among the more affluent.

We have talked for 40 years or more about how education will change everything. Once a girl is educated, everything will be fine. But no one has explained how education will come into the lives of these women. Very often, if there is enough money to send a child to school, it will be the boy who gets preference, not the girl. The girl will stay at home, helping to care for the younger children or tending to the household, so we continue to perpetuate the position of man versus woman. A wife gets ill and dies. Good, we can get more money from a new dowry and another woman. Women are not worth much: the concept of a cared-for life partner is not the norm. Of course, there are many marriages where the men do look after their wives, but even then men do not consider women as they do fellow men.

The slightly surprising point is that this attitude runs right through society in the whole of the sub-continent. People say times are changing, and point to the fact that Indira Gandhi became Prime Minister of India, or Benazir Bhutto became Prime Minister of Pakistan, or Khaleda Zia became Prime Minister of Bangladesh. But they would never have achieved those high positions without their family background and their fathers or husbands holding high office before them. Sonia Gandhi, a reluctant entrant into political life, won her election in 2004 although she turned down the post of Prime Minister. Let's be frank – it is dynastic.

Today some will point to the appointment in India of Pratibha Patil as the first woman President of India as an example of how women can achieve high office, a victory over widespread discrimination. I wonder. Simply choosing a woman because it suits the government's agenda does not do the cause of women any good. The previous incumbent, Dr A. P. J. Abdul Kalam, was too strong-willed for the politicians, a scientist and a visionary. He stood up for himself, and if he disagreed with a policy he would say so. When his term of office was over, they needed someone they could control. Who better than a woman without a track record? This is not a reflection on Pratibha Patil's integrity, just an acknowledgement of the reality that she was generally unknown and without a notable background in public life.

Yes, there are women in minor ministerial positions, but if you talk to them privately they will say that they are treated differently from the men, who almost gang up on them making life, even for someone as important as a government minister, very hard. Occasionally, there is a one-off, as with a lady called Mayawati Kumari. Known just as Mayawati, she is uniting India's ten mainly regional opposition parties. In the 2007 elections in Uttar Pradesh, the most populous state in India, she upset the political status quo when her Bahujan Samaj Party won an outright majority. Not only is she a woman, but she is also from the so-called Untouchables caste, and has been dubbed 'Queen of the Dalits'. The Congress Party, who have traditionally enjoyed the support of the country's 160 million Dalits,[8] are worried – so too is the main Hindu-nationalist opposition party, the BJP (Bharatiya Janata Party.)

India and Africa will be considered more closely, but let me just touch here on the whole question of HIV. There are many monogamous women in the villages who are infected with HIV. The only person who could have infected them is their husband, but they are not allowed to go to the clinics because everyone will then know that their husband is infected. It is accepted that men should be allowed to sleep around. Many of them are lorry drivers, who move about the country, often going with a woman wherever they stop for the night. By contrast, if a woman has illicit sex she would probably be killed. The UN accepts that 70 per cent of the HIV-infected people in the world are women, not men, and that surely tells its own story.

My argument is not that I can change the sexual habits of men overnight, but that if women are given the opportunity to earn a little money they can take better care of themselves. I don't even want to try to get men to behave better towards their wives. I am a realist. But in helping women to look after themselves, I can see a clear social and commercial advantage. Don't just take my word for it. In its Gender Equality and Growth Evidence and Action report, published in February 2008, the UK's

---

8   Sudras or Dalits were the lowest in the Hindu caste hierarchy and treated as untouchables – even looking at them was considered unlucky by the three higher castes: the Brahmin, Kshatriya and Vaishya. The caste system was formally abolished when the Constitution of India was adopted on 26 January 1950.

Department for International Development (DFID) highlighted evidence which clearly showed that 'societies that increase women's access to education, healthcare, employment and credit and that narrow differences between men and women in economic opportunities increase the pace of economic development and reduce poverty'.

I think it is obvious from even this briefest of snapshots that life for women is intolerable, so what is in it for business? We are now global operators. Businesses are not just local to cities or even countries: many of the major ones have links and operations around the world. Employers who wield such international influence should look at their core business, examine exactly what they do and study their supply chains. Their business may reach ten times the number of people they employ directly and, in view of that impact, there may be instances where women could be employed or even be more suited to the work than the men. One has to accept that there is certain employment for which women are not well equipped, but not much: when you see women carrying bricks up and down ladders on building sites, their babies sleeping in the dust and all this in the heat, cold and rain, then you have to accept that they are tough. They have to be to survive. Many have to live on site, finding shelter in pipes or whatever is there. So it is important to see how, not if, a woman can fit into the business. It requires positive thought and a little lateral thinking, otherwise it would be too easy to say there isn't a slot. Businesses are international and constantly evolving: why should it be so difficult for part of that evolution to include women? It may be possible to create a new workshop which would increase business and help the women at the same time. If corporations, large and small, start working along these lines, then change will happen and it will be sustainable. I have no doubt that the concept will snowball once the benefits become apparent, and once the momentum begins there will be no stopping it, because it is logical.

What are the obstacles? There is always a fear of change, and businesses are showing that fear. They are reluctant to look seriously at this option because they fear that they will be accused of discriminating in favour of women. That is one of those notions trotted out when you don't want to try anything to help women. But think of the discrimination against women down the centuries, some of which we have already considered: even if there were discrimination in favour of women, it would not be such a bad thing. The health of a nation would be improved, thereby also improving the quality of future employees because they would be better educated. You would uplift humanity, and that cannot be achieved unless women are uplifted too.

Inertia is a common excuse. If the business is running along fine as it is, why change anything? The problem is too big – is it really worth the effort? I would reply to this: what about the Millennium Development Goals? Every major nation has signed up to the MDGs, and business is not exempt. But what has anyone been seriously doing to achieve those goals? You can't just throw money at them. There has been so much debt reduction in Africa, but where is the evaluation of what this has delivered? It is no good pouring more money into the already engorged Swiss bank accounts – you have to know where the money is going.

Will it work? I have no doubt; and there are some examples we can point to already, albeit largely NGO-led. One of the biggest and best known is the Bangladesh Rural Advancement Committee (BRAC), a development organisation founded by Fazle Hasan Abed in 1972 – an idea that slowly began to form in his mind following the 1970 cyclone. He explained that he felt uncomfortable abandoning the victims once the emergency relief work was over: 'We felt that we could not walk out on these people leaving them to their own devices to fend for themselves. We felt that we needed to commit ourselves to the long-term development of rural Bangladesh – in the provision of education, healthcare, family-planning services, building organisations for the poor – and empower them to demand services from the state. We needed to develop new avenues and work opportunities for our poor people, particularly for our women.'[9]

That initial effort has been broadened to tackle long-term poverty. BRAC's website says: 'Our unique, holistic approach to poverty alleviation and empowerment of the poor encompasses a range of core programmes in economic and social development, health, education, and human rights and legal services. Today, BRAC is the largest southern NGO and employs more than 100,000 people, the majority of which are women, and reaches more than 110 million people with our development interventions in Asia and Africa.'

Also in Bangladesh, we have the innovative work of Professor Muhammad Yunus and his concept of micro-credit. He created the Grameen (Village) banking system, extending credit to the world's poor. Most of the seven million plus beneficiaries to date are women. The first loans Yunus issued were for the equivalent of £14.50 to 42 women in Jobra, a village near Chittagong University in Bangladesh, where he came up with the idea while professor of economics. His lateral thinking broke the rigid mould of conventional banking, which would not allow the poor to get credit without some form of guarantee. It also broke the pernicious stranglehold of local money-lenders who charged exorbitant interest rates.

But even innovative ideas such as micro-credit have a saturation point, so we have to look for new ideas. You can keep going the NGO route, and the NGOs will

---

9   *Asian Enterprise*, Summer 2008.

keep helping, but unless global businesses start playing their part there can be no real progress. My proposal is to start at the top with the truly international operators, in the belief that medium- and small-sized businesses will follow their lead. Put simply, what we want to do is to move towards a situation where women are actually producing goods, and businesses are providing opportunities for work in return for wages and profits.

I believe now is the hour. There has never before been a time when business has had such an enormous role in world affairs. Business can be flexible while governments are rigid and bureaucratic, and consequently slow to respond. Furthermore, there has never been a time when so many major issues have come together at one time: environment, HIV, poverty, energy resources, the economy. If you don't include half the world's population in the solution process, nothing will change. The British Prime Minister, Gordon Brown, said on his return from a trip to Africa that women were the agents of change. I have been visiting projects in Africa, India, Pakistan, Bangladesh and Nepal for the past 17 years and I have not the slightest doubt that women are the agents of change – possibly the only agents of change.

Why am I so convinced? The answer is simple: most women have nothing. When you have nothing, everything, however small, is important. If, as a man, you are brought up from day one to think of yourself as a superior being and everything is available to you, why should you bother to make any effort? Your food will always be there when you come home from work; you will be able to beat your wife if you are angry about something or rape her whenever you feel like it. You can infect her with HIV. What is missing from your life as a man? But what has the woman got? Absolutely nothing, and it is precisely this that makes her so valuable as an agent of change for any business. As soon as you give a poor woman an opportunity, she seizes it with both hands. This is what all NGOs and charities have found. Not only will women make the change happen, but they will do it within weeks, not months or years, if you allow them to generate just a small amount of income for themselves. If you think by sitting women down to teach them literacy you will help, you are wrong. They will not be interested because it has no relevance to their lives; it doesn't provide immediate food for the family, it doesn't help them buy a shirt for their child, it doesn't help them buy medicine to treat infection.

Let me give just one small and very real example. I saw a project where the women were given some embroidery work. Everything they made was sold at special markets. I could tell the reaction. I don't need an interpreter, and could speak directly to these women. They were so upbeat. They had a purpose in life, whereas before they lived without hope. They told me that they used to have to beg their husbands for even one rupee to buy a sweet for their child; now they can provide it themselves.

The change in the women was obvious. They wore brighter clothes, they looked happy and well. And their happiness was infectious. The biggest potential obstacle, of course, was the husbands, but before long there was a grudging acceptance from them that life was getting better. The whole family was better dressed and better fed. You can't really beat your wife for that.

Lest I am misunderstood, this is nothing to do with women's equality or rights or empowerment. Those things will come in due course, and it is not for me to push such an agenda because that would certainly lead to conflict. I want to improve the way women live and, through that, improve the lives of their families, including their husbands.

This is not about the modern approach to women's empowerment; in fact I do not actually agree with that because empowerment in that sense is about creating something for yourself. Such ideas are unsustainable and unrealistic in these circumstances. However, it is clear that if you set women on the road to income generation – economic empowerment rather than personal empowerment – then they will become aware of these other matters in due course, but it is up to them to seek it and not for outsiders to promote or push it.

In India they are learning about rural development ministries, and the importance of the role of village councils and what they can do for themselves. That works well because it is not about a western notion of empowerment. Many women have started taking an interest in what is happening in their local government but it is patchy. If women have aspirations for politics, this is where it should begin, working through the ranks and not being given a family leg-up on the ladder.

So in short, what is the solution I am proposing? I want business to start a series of sustainable initiatives targeting women which will be profitable to the company and generate income for the poor. It is not a five-year plan and it is not about governments promising money that will never reach the neediest. I am looking to the most successful global businesses that have the influence to make this crucial change come about. I have more faith in the ability of go-getters and entrepreneurs to provide the solutions which work best for them. They are the people used to getting results and they are profit-driven. I accept that it might require some lateral thinking, but change only comes about by thinking smartly and differently, not by doing more of the same.

Education and literacy are fine for the future, but for now this is just a dream. The best part of the changes I am proposing is the immediate impact they will have on the women, their children and the company's bottom line.

2

AFRICAN
WOMAN

All the statistics about Africa make staggering reading. There are magnificent statistics about the size of the continent, the wonder of its resources and the beauty of its landscape, and then there are the other facts: the poverty, the hardship, the disease and the brutality. Some 40 per cent of Africans go to bed hungry every single night; a child is said to die every six seconds from disease or poverty; 43 per cent of children in sub-Saharan Africa do not have access to safe drinking water;[10] and children account for half of all civilian casualties in wars in Africa.[11] At the heart of all this misery is mismanagement – mismanagement of the politics, of the economy, of the agriculture, of the business infrastructure. Something has to change.

In general terms, women in Africa work the land while the men gravitate

10 UNICEF.
11 *Africa 2015*.org.

to the cities in search of easier and faster reward, little of which finds its way back to their families in the villages. Agriculture supports about 70 per cent of the population in most African countries, and while women grow 80 per cent of the food and care for the livestock, they own only 1 per cent of the land; worse still, if a husband dies his ownership of the land rarely passes to the widow, so there is no security for her or her children. If a business manager wants to find the perfect example of a multi-tasking employee, he need look no further than the women; their roles are all linked to the success of the economy – child-bearing, management of resources (water, food, fuel and land), management of family finances, education of their children and caring for the elderly. Those who know me, know my mantra: women represent half the population, do three quarters of the work, earn 10 per cent of the wages and own 1 per cent of the property.

I once said to the Nigerian High Commissioner in London that when I have been working hard I say that I have been working like an African woman, and he said I was absolutely correct because there were parts of Nigeria where men just sat under the trees and played ludo or snakes and ladders all day. Of course, this may not be representative of the whole of Nigeria, but the fact remains that women in Africa do the work, and it can start very young.

It is worst for a young girl. Not only is she likely to be undernourished, but while her brothers are outside kicking a football around, she will be looking after the younger children, preparing meals, and when the food is ready she will even wait on the men and boys; when she is not cooking and cleaning she will be fetching and carrying the firewood and water because, in all probability, her mother will be lying in bed too ill with HIV to help. And I am not talking about teenage girls here; a girl as young as eight would be expected to shoulder the burdens of the family. I recall a BBC documentary of a young girl with an even younger sister and three boys – one her brother and two nephews – her mother was too ill to help. The boys played all day while the girl ran the home and got the medicine for her mother as well as all the other fetching, carrying and cleaning. I remember her sitting down with her head in her hands and saying: 'Life is terrible.' That picture will haunt me for the rest of my life. How can this keep on happening? Why should this girl child be the slave to everyone? Nothing is expected of the boys. When this girl finally lies down on her mat at night, exhausted and hungry, I wonder what she dreams about; I wonder if she even understands that she can have any hopes and dreams.

Many of the women who are not in the cities are alone even if they are married because, apart from the few men who do help farm the land, the rest are in the towns and cities looking for work. When the men eventually return home, all that happens is the women become pregnant again and they soon have another mouth to feed;

they have to cope with all this single-handedly, along with water shortages, food and fuel shortages, Aids and sometimes even war as well.

In times of conflict, the women again are usually worst affected. They have to protect the children if they can, they get raped – a common weapon of war – and are brutalised in every way. Wars have been raging in different parts of Africa for centuries. The fighting in the Democratic Republic of Congo in November 2008 was just one of the latest to hit the headlines – 1,500 were dying there every day according to a survey by the International Rescue Committee. But one could also mention conflicts in neighbouring Rwanda or the Sudan, Zimbabwe, Ethiopia, and the list goes on. Twenty-eight wars have been fought in sub-Saharan Africa since the 1970s. All the evidence suggests that the cause of most if not all wars in Africa has little if anything to do with ethnic or tribal differences – those are just the methodologies for carrying them out. The real cause is greed and the intoxicating allure of fabulous wealth; can we really be surprised if wars are fought when the prize, the chance to escape absolute poverty, is control of mineral-rich land and the sparkle of diamonds or gold? Whatever the cause, the victims are always the same: the weak and innocent, and the weakest and most innocent are the children and women.

Life in the towns and rural communities is different, but both have their hardships. In the towns men and women find jobs, but they may have to be separated from their families or travel for two or three hours from the shanty towns to work. Men who work in the mines, for example, live in hostels, while the women in towns, in all probability, will have left their children behind in the care of their parents or other relatives in their home villages. These living conditions seem to heighten the complete absence of sexual morality. It goes without saying that there is a lot of promiscuity; girls become pregnant very early in their lives. But apart from consensual sex there is a huge incidence of rape, to the extent that almost every girl can expect to be raped. It is almost the norm and, of course, HIV/Aids is rampant. I have seen the awful conditions in the townships around Johannesburg. It need not be this way, but change requires concerted effort and leadership; it can work, as we have witnessed in Uganda. What I am saying is that women are worth something, but who is brave enough to stand up for them?

Dr Mahmoud Fathalla, Professor of Obstetrics and Gynaecology at Assiut University in Egypt and a former Director of the WHO Special Programme of Research, Development and Research Training in Human Reproduction, was quoted in the Marie Stopes International (MSI)[12] annual review back in 2003: 'Women are not dying because of diseases we cannot treat … they are dying because societies have

---

12   Marie Stopes International is the UK's leading provider of sexual and reproductive health care. www.mariestopes.org.uk

yet to make the decision that their lives are worth saving.' Has anything changed since then? In the same review MSI said: 'Every minute of every day a woman dies from a pregnancy-related cause. Every ninth death is the result of an unsafe abortion. When mothers die, or when births occur less than three years apart, babies are more than twice as likely to die.' I have been to the Marie Stopes clinics in Cape Town and seen for myself the constant battle they are fighting on behalf of women. According to UNICEF, in 2005 there were 536,000 maternal deaths worldwide and of those about half were in sub-Saharan Africa. The risk of maternal death in the developing world is 1 in 76 compared with 1 in 8,000 in the industrialised world.

Of all the problems Africa faces, the greatest is undoubtedly the huge growth in population. While Europe is anticipating a 14 per cent fall in its overall population by 2050, Africa is likely to witness an increase of 130 per cent according to the UN Population Division. Nigeria on its own looks set to become the third most populous country in the world after China and India. In its excellent report in July 2008, the House of Lords Select Committee on Intergovernmental Organisations tackled the issue of how effective such organisations are in stopping the spread of disease, and highlighted the impact of the rise in population:

> Population growth is now, however, itself threatening global health by cre-
> ating conditions, such as urbanisation and overcrowding, where infectious
> disease can spread more easily, especially where basic public health services,
> such as clean water and sanitation, are not available. In some parts of the world
> rising populations are also leading to increasing encroachment on previously
> uninhabited areas of land, both for agriculture and habitation, and thereby
> bringing humans into closer contact with wild animals and exposing them to
> pathogens to which they have no immunity and which can jump the species
> barrier and infect then with previously unknown illnesses. It is no exaggera-
> tion to say that a continuance of present rates of population increase threatens
> the achievement of most, if not all, the MDGs.[13]

One of those who gave evidence to the committee, Professor Janet Hemingway, of the Liverpool School of Tropical Medicine, put the argument for earning capacity as an essential to health succinctly:

> Health benefits go hand in hand with economic development; there is no
> question about that … Unless there is something that tackles poverty along-
> side health systems, you are fighting a losing battle in many ways.

Population growth and how to manage it are central to everything, and I shall make no apologies for returning to it throughout this book. How can it be right for a woman

---

13 *Diseases Know No Frontiers: How effective are Intergovernmental Organisations in controlling their spread?* Volume 1. Report, House of Lords Select Committee on Intergovernmental Organisations, 21 July 2008.

who is already starving and probably ill to have yet another child when she cannot feed the mouths around her already? It is not good for the mother and certainly not good for the baby, who will be condemned to a life of hunger and suffering. Rather than see another desperate face looking with pleading eyes into the TV cameras as well-meaning charities try to raise more funds, surely it would be better if women had fewer babies? All those organisations offering aid to the starving should also be offering help to women so they don't have another baby in nine months' time.

The population growth may be central, but we keep dodging the issue and we need to be reminded of the urgency. In one of its recommendations the Select Committee called on the British Government to 'support and contribute to an increase in resources being allocated to family planning throughout the developing world'. We have vilified China for having a one-child policy, but when we see the change that has come about in China, do we really think they would have succeeded without adopting such drastic measures? I realise, of course, that in a democracy you cannot order women to have only one child, but I am suggesting that we should help them stop having four, five or more children, for their own well-being, for their children's future and yes, for the well-being of the planet. When Mao said that China's strength lay in its people, they were having six or seven children; yet without a one-child policy would they have been in the dominant position they are in today?

There has been a further consequence of this tough policy: families living in the towns are happier because they can focus their efforts on one child who can achieve even more, to the extent that there are now more Chinese students able to study abroad than from any other nation. However, China has recognised the danger of having an aging population, and when two single children get married they can have two children without suffering any financial penalties. The law, which is restricted to the ethnic Han Chinese in urban areas, has reduced the population growth by a staggering 400 million people since it was imposed some 30 years ago.

In a presentation to the UK Parliament addressing population issues, Professor J. Joseph Speidel of the Department of Obstetrics, Gynecology and Reproductive Sciences at the University of California said: 'Recent studies examining the Asian economic "tigers" and other rapidly advancing economies strongly suggest that improved health and a decreased dependency ratio – a result of rapid declines in fertility – provide countries with a "demographic bonus" that can foster economic growth.'[14]

I agreed with the advice of Sir Jonathon Porritt, the Labour Government's green guru, when he called for British couples to have smaller families. He was reported

---

14 Presentation to the UK All Party Parliamentary Group on Population, Development and Reproductive Health, 26 June 2006.

as saying it was 'irresponsible' of parents to have more than two children.[15] The former Green Party member and now chairman of the government's Sustainable Development Commission went further when he accused other environmentalists of 'betraying' their cause by shying away from openly calling for people to limit the number of children they have. Despite the immediate condemnation, it is an issue which cannot be ignored.

Earlier, to coincide with World Population Day on 11 July 2008, the Optimum Population Trust published a study questioning our unlimited right to have children. It said: 'Most of us consider the decision of whether to have children an entirely personal matter. The thought of others being affected or having a say in the decision strikes us as an interference with our privacy. In reality, it is the most public action – in the sense of influencing the lives of others – most citizens will ever take.' It went on to say: 'Only the decision not to have children is a genuinely private act. Not procreating is personal; procreating is interpersonal.'[16]

Africa can never become like China and have a one-child policy; for a start, it is a continent and not ruled by a single power, but it is fair to say that China would not have made such rapid strides without such a dictatorial regime. Having said that, I question China's motives for investing so heavily in Africa: is it to reduce the influence of other players in the region enabling China to establish and consolidate their own foothold? Their approach to Darfur is hideous because they refused to join other governments in the UN Security Council in condemning Khartoum for the genocide that was being perpetrated in the Sudan. It seems that the improvement of the lives of Africans is not their prime motive. And no one should be surprised; they are hardly likely to put humanitarian rights above mineral riches and oil reserves. That 200,000 or more people have been killed and 2.5 million displaced are merely unpalatable statistics. To put it bluntly, China wants Sudan's oil and Sudan wants China's dollars.

One may not think that the daily grind of the average rural African woman has much bearing on our comfortable lives in the western world, but it does: as she scratches away at her small piece of land, she gradually erodes the local habitat and has to walk further afield in search of firewood and water. What will Ethiopians do when, come 2020, they have no natural forests left?[17] The poor woman cannot afford the luxury of worrying about the environmental impact of desertification; she has to light

---

15 *Daily Telegraph*, 2 February 2009.

16 The Optimum Population Trust is the leading think tank in the UK concerned with the impact of population growth on the environment.

17 Report compiled for the UN's Emergencies Unit for Ethiopia citing human interference mainly for subsistence and economic reasons as the most important cause of desertification.

a fire to cook the food. The western liberal notion that it doesn't matter how many children such a mother might have is an illogical approach because it takes no account of the real impact of each and every life. The poor only consume less because they have less, and slowly but surely they will spread out in search of more, leaving behind them a barren landscape stripped of nutrients, destroying their own environment.

This destruction should not have to happen in countries rich in resources. But I am not so naive as to think that oil revenues of somewhere like Nigeria will suddenly find their way to the masses, so my approach is different. I am not asking for any of those billions of dollars; I am focused on the few cents which could be derived from a slight variation in corporate strategies. If a woman is capable of achieving so much with nothing, consider what she could achieve with a little.

Africa is obviously a business opportunity – why else would China be there? – and it is a continent rich in resources which are already being exploited by large, international corporations. In a curious twist of economic good fortune following the financial turmoil of 2008/9, these underdeveloped countries have an opportunity. As Professor Paul Collier, author of the prize-winning best-seller *The Bottom Billion* (Oxford University Press) and director of the Centre for the Study of African Economics at Oxford University, pointed out in one article, because the low-income economies of the world were 'never sufficiently creditworthy to benefit from substantial private credit during the wild, late phase of irrational exuberance … African banks are not stuffed with toxic assets and opaque derivatives and so they have not been dragged down.'[18] He added: 'Gradual but cumulatively substantial policy reform coupled with debt relief now means most of these economies are in much better shape than a decade ago.'

Despite its record of wars, corruption and poor governance, Africa will remain attractive to businesses for years to come, so we have to think how we can bring about change for the good of the people. It is not sufficient for business to conclude that a growing population necessarily means more customers – particularly if so many of them are sick or starving or both. Business has to accept some responsibility for its customer base, and they should definitely take care of their potential future employees.

There are initiatives such as Opportunity International, who work not only in Africa and Asia but also in Eastern Europe and Latin America, providing micro-finance to people who would normally have no access to banking facilities such as loans and insurance. Interestingly, they use a slightly different model for the society in which they are working – in other words, they look at local conditions and apply

---

18   Paul Collier. 'A Less Developed Crunch', *Prospect*, Issue 156, 1 March 2009.

them. So they have taken the African model of having a group and choosing a group leader. If someone falls by the wayside, collectively the group helps that person get back on their feet. It is successful precisely because it adapts to the local customs. In the same way, what I am proposing is not to force everyone into a classroom to become literate, but first to help them at their level: provide families with a means to survive by focusing on the mother, and then when they have acquired the basic essentials of life they will be able to get something out of education, which first and foremost should be basic literacy. But for every successful initiative, there are dozens of failures. Well-meaning fund-raising events struggle to make the money reach those who need it most; foundations are established, but all too often they are just window dressing without any real desire for change in the long term, or established for tax evasion purposes.

It is important to stress that I am not trying to change society in Africa or the sub-continent in terms of equality, or somehow putting men down. The central point which I will keep coming back to is that if women have access to opportunity and are ready for change then they will bring about change in society themselves. It is not for others to tell them what they should do. Those changes will quickly lead first to poverty alleviation, then to better health and education for their children. It will also be up to the women to decide how far-reaching those changes should be. But all these benefits can only come about when, as an individual, a woman has a stronger sense of her ability to do something, a sense of self-worth. Unless you can make somebody feel that they are capable, you cannot change anything. If you have half the population serving the rest who have demonstrated that they are incapable of changing anything, then is it not time to give that half a chance to show what they can do? We must not allow the sort of widespread subsistence farming which exists throughout Africa to continue, not only for the benefit of those farming families but also for the rest of us, as already explained. The right thing is to encourage some form of farming cooperatives, but that requires government intervention and I know how unlikely that can be.

The tragic irony is that although most of Africa's population is involved in some way in agriculture, the continent cannot feed its own rapidly growing and increasingly undernourished population and is forced to bring in some $20 billion of food imports in addition to the $2 billion it receives in food aid from the United States. And there is a negative impact to those very imports: the so-called food import surges are actually putting local producers out of business as their own margins are cut. The growing population needs more jobs not fewer, so this policy is not the answer. Even food aid has had a negative impact in parts of Africa where people now rely totally on aid; they seem to have forgotten how to work and instead just wait for the next food handout. What kind of future generations are we helping to create if no one is doing anything to provide long-term solutions?

It is clear, therefore, that you cannot rely on politicians and governments who seem to be more concerned about staying in power at all costs rather than helping their own people. There are no civil institutions that are strong enough to run matters properly. What stands out in Africa as a model of good governance? So we have to look to the individuals themselves. You cannot understand how people exist when you see the distressing images of utter impoverishment. Ten years hence, where will we be? The answer is heading inexorably towards disaster. How can anyone realistically believe that a single one of the Millennium Development Goals can be met by the target date? I will look at these goals in more detail later (see Chapter 6). Worthy though they are, they will never be achieved in the timescale suggested. In truth I am frightened for the world and glad that I will not be around to witness what might happen in a few short decades.

I am not asking for outside assistance in the form of finance. I am advocating that businesses should provide the opportunity for impoverished people to do precisely what organisations like UNCTAD (United Nations Conference on Trade and Development) suggested in 2007 that Africa should do – help itself. It advised that Africa should follow the likes of Korea and Taiwan, which have managed to grow without any foreign help, and incidentally did so with women being totally integrated into the workforce. There is no other choice since, according to Oxfam, aid budgets to the continent are actually falling overall and the current financial squeeze will inevitably lead to a drop in aid.[19]

Although I don't think aid and handouts are the answer, continuing support in the short term is, of course, essential. Despite the squeeze there seemed to be plenty of money to prop up failing banks as countries around the world launched so-called stimulus packages of unheard of proportions. But the World Bank had another thought. The bank's Managing Director, Dr. Ngozi Okonjo-Iweala, a former Finance and Foreign Minister in Nigeria, warned leaders of the G20 developed and emerging nations as they were about to meet for a conference in London that cutting aid to poor countries during the global recession could trigger a 'monumental' human crisis.[20] Okonjo-Iweala urged them to promise 0.7 per cent of their recovery packages for a fund to help the poorest nations because failure to help them could lead to widespread unrest. Developing nations, she said, would have a 'lost global generation' with up to 2.8 million more infant deaths by 2015. She said: 'It is a matter

---

19 Oxfam received £290 million from British donations in 2008 and was expecting 'zero growth' in donations in 2009. They were planning staff cuts to keep costs down (*Daily Telegraph*, 8 November 2008).

20 Peter Griffiths, 'World Bank seeks more G20 aid for world's poorest', *Reuters*, 9 March 2009.

of self-preservation for the developed world and of life and death for the developing world.'

Dr. Okonjo-Iweala's boss, Robert Zoellick, who was appointed to head the World Bank from his post as Managing Director of Goldman Sachs, went further a few days later when he forecast more bad news for the global economy – 'growth will fall about 1pc to 2pc' – and added: 'So these are serious and dangerous times.'[21]

Chief executives will argue that business already accepts that it must do more. Every company now recognises that it has a corporate social responsibility. They do indeed, but I fear that in many cases it is just a smokescreen behind which corporations hide to prove that they are doing something for society. They do a little because it is fashionable and only just enough to keep the environmentalists quiet. It is both a minimalist and short-termist approach. I recall attending a meeting of the much-touted UN Commission for Africa where I suggested to an African Commissioner that women should be seen as working partners in creating the success of a country as they are in Korea and Taiwan and other Far Eastern countries, and he actually laughed in my face at the concept and said it would not be acceptable to men.

In their article on industrial development and social responsibility, Odd Henrik Robberstad, Senior Vice President Corporate Social Responsibility for Norsk Hyrdo, and Professor Rolf Lunheim, a corporate anthropologist for Norsk Hydro, which operates in some 40 different countries, said: 'It is imperative that the participants in the business world recognise the necessity and long-term self-interest of self-imposed ethical rules and social responsibility.' And this is precisely the point, business must not think of this as a burden or a distraction to their day-to-day activity, but an essential aspect of everything they do; in time a small 'investment' in the local community – and I would advocate that it should be in women to guarantee the best return – will pay substantial dividends.

The late Lord Holme of Cheltenham CBE, when a member of the World Business Council for Sustainable Development and co-chairman of its Working Party on Corporate Social Responsibility, said: 'Any company which is seriously misaligned with the hopes and fears of its fellow citizens in society is likely to pay a price in lost reputation or sales for getting out of step.'

The impact of even a small initiative can reach far beyond the project itself, as Brian Donaldson, the former British Ambassador to Madagascar, points out in this story about a single bridge. He explains how the erstwhile Small Grants Scheme (SGS) of the Foreign Office allowed him to fund the construction of a 14-metre concrete bridge over a steep-sided river:

---

21   Alex Brummer. 'City Interview: Worst is yet to come, says World Bank boss', *Daily Mail*, 11 March 2009.

The bridge had been planned in 1962, when local authorities built the first supporting pillar. Although funding for the project had been provided several times, it had been stolen repeatedly by corrupt officials.

To reach the nearest primary school, children waded through chest-high water, then spent the school day in wet clothes. Often the river was impassable at the end of the day and the children were unable to return home. Farmers, too, were handicapped by the absence of a bridge. Because of the difficulty of transporting their produce to market they were forced to sell to 'collectors' – middle-men who paid unfairly low prices, but who owned trucks that could navigate the river to reach otherwise inaccessible markets.

SGS funded construction of the bridge at a cost of £3,500. Today the children attend school and return home dry and safe each night; farmers transport their own produce to market and receive a fair price for their labours; and the communities on either side of the river are united as never before.[22]

People speak of the triple bottom line – financial results, social and biological environment – but who is going to hold companies to account? Companies follow the law – ensuring there are clean emissions and low pollution – but there is no legal requirement for companies to actually do anything specific to help the local communities. Programmes that do exist are patchy and haphazard, and there is no way of evaluating those triple bottom lines and comparing one company with another. Social and biological responsibility should be more than putting up signs in factories about the risk of HIV/Aids or guidance on family planning.

Across Africa where there are large truck stops, should they not consider properly organised and cared for brothels and advice centres? But if you talk about such things people get worked up. Why? The aim is to reduce disease, educate people about HIV and family planning, and the net result is a healthier and more thriving community, which in turn means a thriving economy. The facts are startling: in developing countries it is estimated that the average fertility rate among 15–19-year-olds is more than five times greater than in more developed countries.[23]

I return to my African woman struggling in the fields and her husband working away from home, perhaps in a mine or factory, inexorably drifting apart, living lives of subsistence with no hope of breaking out of the spiral of decline. Initiative after initiative has failed. I have attended debates, corporate governance conferences where seemingly impossible targets are set, but we never mention half the population – women. Surely there is now a compelling argument to say everything else has been tried, nothing has worked, why not see if the other half of the population can do better?

22   Brian Donaldson. *Think Small: The Example of Small Grants in Madagascar*, Africa Research Institute, 2008.

23   Guttmacher Institute 2006.

African women are no different in one sense to women the world over; they are the ones who take prime responsibility for health care in the family, whether a child has a small accident or whether there is a disease like malaria or hepatitis. Family planning is always up to the woman; so too is preparing the meals, maintaining the household whether it is a shack in a refugee camp or a house in the city. The message I am trying to put across to businesses is that women are a formidable, resilient, reliable and effective workforce; they have to be, because there is no one else to turn to. If a company just takes a fraction of that energy and applies it in a small way to their business, imagine what the impact will be. The balance has been wrong since time began and it is time to change – for all our sakes.

3

INDIAN WOMAN

The greatest obstacle to overcome is that life is too comfortable for men; and nowhere is life better for men than in India. Let's face it, if you can be paid to marry a young girl who will serve you and your family night and day and hardly expect anything in return, why should a man want to change his life? Whatever resources are available, man always has first claim. They don't have to worry about the basics of life: their food is cooked, their children are looked after and they have no responsibility for any of those things. After all, they work so hard they should be allowed to get drunk and gamble and have a bit of fun. And on Saturday nights they should be allowed to beat their wives; they see it almost as their right!

But first let's compare their life with life in Africa. The contrast is enormous in so many ways, and yet, in some, depressingly the same. The impression of India now is that the country is booming, the economy is racing ahead, and India is a force to be reckoned with – all of which is true. Africa seems incapable of running itself in any meaningful or stable fashion despite its natural wealth. But strip away some of the economic gloss of India, step out of the glitz and the high-rise buildings and air-conditioned, five star hotels, and you very quickly see a nation which is struggling to catch up. Someone described India as being like a big snake with its head moving into the 21st century and its tail still in the 16th. Just as in Africa, shouldering the burdens and ensuring families get through each and every day is the woman's role, and in India the dominance of man has been inculcated into every walk of life – work, the home, religion. But it was not always that way.

Without going too deeply into the complexities of Hinduism, male and female gods and goddesses are seen as complementary. If you study the myths and icons, the male deities are made complete only by their female consorts. Without that force or energy known as the *Shakti*, the god will not have complete power; so Parvati provides the energy for Shiva, Lakshmi for Vishnu. The goddesses can be depicted as strong, even ferocious, like Kali with skulls round her neck or, in a different form as a warrior, as Durga sitting astride a tiger brandishing a sword.

The importance of the feminine is clear: we speak of Mother India. At the annual Diwali celebrations, which have now become common in the West, attended and respected by international politicians, Lakshmi receives the praise and her husband does not come into the celebration. So with all this devotion, what has changed between the temple and the home? All is forgotten. Where did it all go wrong?

I would argue that the story of Rama, the seventh incarnation of Vishnu and the key figure in the much-vaunted Ramayana Hindu epic, [24] and his treatment of his wife, Sita – whose virtue was questioned, sending her into exile even though she was pregnant at the time – has done nothing to help the cause of women. Perhaps the rot, if I may call it that, set in with the book of the Hindu code *Manavardharma Sastra* – The Laws of Manu, the ancient lawgiver of the first century. The code stipulated that women were subordinate and dependent on their fathers until marriage, on their husbands after marriage, and even when widowed on their sons thereafter. It is even possible for a girl to be widowed before actually being old enough to consummate the marriage: if a girl is married to a boy, she will not be expected to go to his house until puberty. But should the boy die first, the girl becomes a widow and under strict religious rules should not 'marry' again.

The treatment of Hindu widows has been appalling. My great-grandfather, Sir Ganga Ram (1851–1927), campaigned for better treatment of unmarried mothers

---

24   The Ramayana epic is the story of Rama, the personification of a virtuous man, and how an ideal man is supposed to behave and a king to rule.

and Hindu widows, creating shelters for them and even having the foresight back then to realise that they needed to have some work which provided an income. I am proud to be able to quote from his biography this short passage about his funeral:

> And most moving of all were the widows, who came out of their sad homes and wept and threw themselves in the path of the precious relics. Their friend, their helper, the one who had wept with them was gone, and they feared that never again would they find a heart so child-like and so gentle to sympathise with their wrongs.[25]

He would be appalled to know that not much has changed since his death in 1927. Until recently widows were still expected to shave their heads, wear distinctive white saris and died unrecognised, unremembered and often in abject poverty. The explanation is that a woman's identity somehow belongs to the man. If he is no longer alive then his widow ceases to exist as an individual; she is also seen as the originator of misfortune. There is even a pilgrimage city in northern India called Vrindavan, which has become the home to thousands of destitute widows reduced to begging for their meals, sometimes literally singing for their supper at temples; if they lose their voice, they don't eat. Widowhood remains a curse, and India is said to have about 40 million widows, the largest number of any country in the world.

Even in some modern and 'sophisticated' households, women still do not sit down and eat with the men and boys of the household. The men eat first, and in the poorest households the women may go hungry. It is even noted that infant girls are likely to receive less breast milk than their brothers and consequently start life undernourished. In short, women become second-class citizens at birth.

It is fair to say that in the major cities it is recognised that women work and, depending on their education, that could mean anything from being a domestic servant to being a teacher, lawyer or politician. Indeed the most educated women in India do well because by and large the overt prejudice holding women back in their careers is more subtle and does not seem to prevail or at least is not obvious, although they do still have to fight every step of the way.

Another reason for their subjugation has been the many invasions of India, from the north in particular, and the influence of the Muslims. With the Muslims came the introduction of Purdah, the practice of the physical segregation of the sexes or of women covering their bodies to conceal themselves when in public. But I wonder for whose benefit all these man-made rules and rituals were introduced? If a woman were to travel on a bus in, say, the Punjab in the north and a man sat down beside her,

---

25   Baba Pyare Lal Bedi. *Harvest from the Desert: The Life and Work of Sir Ganga Ram*, NCA Publications 2003 (reprint).

he would inevitably try and squeeze up against her. In southern India, where there is no Purdah, no Muslim influence, the man on the bus would try not to touch her. So much for morals and fine religious principles.

Not only are Muslim girls shielded physically, but they are also shielded from knowledge and education – this is a trait wherever they are found in the world despite the efforts of many. Unlike in India, it is rare to find great female intellectuals in the Islamic culture, whereas Indian women intellectuals were allowed, even expected, to participate in the mainstream culture and great philosophical debates. Every schoolchild learns about Gargi, the female mathematician. For most Muslim women, education remains elusive. A charity called Arpana established informal groups in villages to teach literacy, but they have failed to get Muslim girls to come because their parents would not allow it. In an attempt to overcome the 'difficulty' of getting the daughters to school, Arpana offered to teach small groups in their own homes. But again the parents refused. The only conceivable reason was to deprive their daughters of a broad education. Too much knowledge, it seems, can be a dangerous thing in some people's eyes.

But I must be fair, because there are 'enlightened' Muslim sects who make education a priority for both sexes: the Ismailis, led by the Aga Khan, the Khojas and the Bohra community are three examples. They all pride themselves on their education and being inclusive, so why do some of the others take such an intolerant line towards women? There are parts of India where women do have equal rights and it has not brought ruin on the community. The most famous example is the south-western state of Kerala, which historically was a matriarchal society. When a couple married, it was the boy who would come and live in the girl's home rather than the other way round, and if he misbehaved he would soon be sent packing by his mother-in-law. The senior female in the household or extended compound – the *tarawad* – was the final arbiter in all matters.

As a result of this system, what you now find in Kerala is a state with almost 100 per cent literacy, where women hold jobs at all levels and can move around without fear. And yet, under matriarchal authority the men were not treated as inferior. They were fierce warriors, but not in the home. The point, of course, is that it is perfectly possible for men and women to live together as equals and for a community to thrive. There are not many parts of the world which can boast 100 per cent literacy, and none where it is traditional to trace the first letter of the alphabet on the infant's tongue as a sign of the great importance they place on education.

The structure began to change when the British arrived and matriarchy was deemed to be backward. It was later, after Independence in 1947, that the Hindu Code Bill – including monogamous marriage – was introduced, provoking fierce reaction at the time. At one stage Jawaharlal Nehru withdrew his support for the bill, provoking his new Minister of Law, B.R. Ambedkar, to resign, saying: 'To leave untouched the inequality between class and class, between sex and sex, and to go on passing legislation relating to economic problems is to make a farce of our Constitution and to build a palace on a dung-heap'.[26] But, as there were soon fewer wars for the men to go off and fight, they stayed at home and became better educated. The result was the break-up of the extended matriarchal homes, and for the first time in Kerala there was homelessness. In more modern times the men began travelling further afield in search of better incomes, and there is a division today between those richer households where the husbands send money back and those in which husbands stayed at home. I wonder if it is just a coincidence that the end of matriarchal rule marked the end of economic and social stability in the state? It is now communist-controlled and there is an increase in union power. The threat of strikes has also resulted in a tailing-off of investment and a greater reliance on funds being remitted by those working outside the state, mainly in the Middle East.

In Kerala when a daughter is born, there is still rejoicing; in the past there would have been more rejoicing for the birth of a girl than a boy, but that brings me to India's darkest crime – the abortion of female foetuses. For all the small wonders of a place like Kerala, where the whole state has been lifted up because of its treatment of women, we have to face the fact that culturally women have always been treated as a sub-species, particularly in the sub-continent. Women are not wanted; they are a burden because parents still have to pay a dowry despite legislation banning the practice.

The British medical journal *The Lancet* reported in 2006 that probably as many as ten million female foetuses – 1 in 25 – had been aborted in India in the previous decade. Although sex determination is illegal under the Pre-Diagnostic Techniques Act, doctors still regularly tell prospective parents whether they are expecting a son or a daughter. The affluent and well-educated are able to buy the US-patented gender testing kit, the Baby Gender Mentor, on the Internet for a mere $275. With roughly one million female foeticides per annum, it is developing into a thriving business for doctors with some estimates saying the operations are generating about Rs 10 billion per annum (£134 million).

The result is that some states in India are running out of women – a friend told me of the rejoicing in one village in Rajasthan where they recently received their first bridegroom's party in 26 years because there had been no girls left alive to marry. In parts of Haryana, a state in northern India, there are about 770 girls for

---

26   Martha Craven Nussbaum. *Woman and Human Development*, Cambridge University Press, 2001.

every 1,000 boys and the consequence of this is an increase in female trafficking; 100,000 women were sold in 2002, according to UN figures. So girls from other states and even from outside the country, known as *paros*, are much in demand. The poorest families facing starvation are selling their own daughters, reversing the dowry system. They might accept $50 if it means finding food to survive – the price is higher if the girl is younger. Initially they may be sold as brides, but all too often they are then 'traded' like some commodity into sex work or as slaves. Brothers have even been known to 'share' a woman, such is the scarcity of eligible girls in some places.

It strikes me that it is utterly tragic and demeaning that a state like Haryana should declare 2006 as Girl Child Year, and consider offering an incentive equivalent to $100 per year for five years if a family has a second daughter. And if a family only had a daughter or daughters, the state would pay them in effect an old-age allowance of $7 per month. To my way of thinking that is almost as bad a trafficking. It is putting a price on a human's head, and worse, it is emphasising the supposed inferiority of females by saying families need extra help to cope with the 'burden' of having a daughter.

This is the starting point from which society has to climb if it really wants to call itself civilised. You cannot put a price tag on women, but we do. I have barely mentioned the iniquitous caste system because that is another debate. But even among the lowest caste, the Dalits, there is a hierarchy which keeps women down. I recall that the only speech I have ever made in Hindi was at a conference organised by Dalits, and I started by saying: 'I see all the brothers here, but where are the sisters? And I told them you ask for equality and fair treatment, but if you cannot give it to your own women how dare you ask for it for yourselves?' That didn't go down too well inside the hall. But all the women, who of course had been kept outside in the gardens, mobbed me when I went out and wanted to touch my feet. I asked them: 'Haven't you heard anything I have said? We are all the same. If you touch my feet I will have to touch yours, so don't do it because I can't bend down easily.'

The glass ceiling can be broken. The politician I have mentioned, Mayawati Kumari, seemed, for a time, to be taking the country by storm. Unmarried and a Dalit herself, she won the vote of the Dalits. I applaud her success, but I wonder how much she is saying specifically about the Dalit women. She does not want to shout too loudly because she needs the support of the Dalit men. I suppose I should not be surprised, when women get into power, that they want to keep it, and they cannot do that by espousing the cause of women; they can only do it by placating the men. Sadly, Mayawati's popularity seems to be in decline. Her state remains one of the poorest in India and shows little sign of improvement under her administration.

Is there a willingness to change man's domination in the sub-continent? It won't happen in my lifetime, but maybe there are glimmers of hope. One personal anecdote I can provide to illustrate the point happened to me in 2008. I was contacted by the Ministry of Overseas Indian Affairs and asked to send some background information about myself because they were considering awarding me the Pravasi Bharatiya Samman. It is a prestigious honour bestowed by the President of India on people who have made an 'exceptional or meritorious contribution' to society in their field. The gentleman who called me said 'We are going off the beaten track this time', meaning a woman was being considered. I said to him: 'I beat track – the first Asian woman in the House of Lords, first woman Mayor of Windsor, and I built a memorial in the heart of London to the Indian soldiers who had volunteered to fight for Britain. You don't get any more of a beaten track.' It was, of course, a great honour to be asked, and for that I am grateful. Perhaps the tone of the request was a little grudging, but I am more than happy to accept small mercies if they are a sign of greater things to come. How sad, though, that news such as this should come at about the same time that we were reading about the appalling so-called honour killings in Baluchistan in Pakistan.

In August 2008 five women, three teenagers and two middle-aged women, were found buried alive, apparently by tribesmen of the Umrani tribe, because the teenagers had refused the tribal leader's arrangements for marriage and insisted on marrying men they loved. The two elder women were their mothers, and presumably backed their daughters. Stunningly, when a woman senator stood up in the national Parliament to condemn the murders, another senator, Israrullah Zehri, now the postal minister, defended the action, saying these were centuries-old traditions, and urged his fellow parliamentarians not to 'highlight them negatively'. Apparently this crime was only carried out because the men had so much 'respect' for women that they could not allow them to live in this state of shame. Only three other members managed to condemn the killings, while the rest kept silent. We shouldn't be surprised by Pakistan: another 2008 appointment, Mir Hazar Khan Bijarani, the new education minister, was reported to have presided over a tribal assembly where five girls were offered as compensation in a murder case.[27] Then in November 2008 the President himself, Asif Ali Zardari, gave a stern lecture to the UN Assembly, saying: 'Bigotry manifested in Islamophobia and anti-Semitism must be combated.' You have to wonder where such a disregard for female life comes in his understanding of bigotry.

We are living in the 21st century, and people elected to national parliaments are still able to acquiesce to such barbarity against another human, dressing it up as a

---

27 *The News* (Karachi).

defence against obscene behaviour. But where is the obscenity – falling in love with a man of one's own choosing or burying girls alive?

You might think I am straying too far from my brief of persuading business to provide work for women, but unless the scene is set and the background understood, there can never be progress. This is the world in which we are living and working. We have to understand what is happening to our customer base. How else can we expect them to buy more? It would be a start if half the potential buyers had a little more money, and once they did were able to live a life free from fear. Don't think this is all too remote from Britain's leafy suburbs. I had to look after some money for a woman living near me in the UK because her husband took the money she earned and beat her for good measure. He even had the gall to keep his mistress in the same house. Eventually, after years of suffering, she managed to get a divorce. I wonder what the mistress herself was thinking. What sort of existence was she having? The misery women dish out to other women is another matter, and I will look at it more closely later, but it is a well-known fact that when women marry and in due course become mothers-in-law themselves, many feel it is their turn to take it out on their daughters-in-law. After all, they seem to argue, we suffered as newly weds: why shouldn't our daughters-in-law?

All this abuse and suffering is going on under our noses, and I wonder why men do not get more worked up about the treatment their fellow males are handing out. Unless they do so, nothing will change. I want business leaders to think for just a moment about the community they serve because I firmly believe that the power of global commerce alone will be able to make the difference. There could not be a better opportunity for change, particularly in India, than there is today: in Asia, only China has more billionaires than India, according to *Forbes Magazine*. There are companies increasingly involving women, but they are not always bringing them into the business mainstream, which has to be the ultimate goal, even if only in a small way initially, in order for real change to happen. Actually I have a recurring nightmare about all the wealth that is spinning round in the financial markets: I see the money circling the globe and never actually touching the ground to create any benefit for people. Only the super-rich Indian billionaires and the financial traders in the money markets seem to benefit, but once they have their cars and their houses and their yachts, what will they do then? They have to create work for the people – all the people. Perhaps they could start competing with each other over who could achieve more in helping the disadvantaged?

Everything that people are doing to help women – in the NGO sectors, for instance – is to be applauded, but until women are seen as a workforce the groundswell will not start. If they perform well then the change will come. If a business hasn't got anything suitable then devise some small subsidiary division that does and make money out it. But above all don't do it as a charity, because until people understand that the solution has to be found away from charity and move to the reality of making money – yes, out of women – nothing will happen.

This should not be considered an exclusively Indian company responsibility. Most major companies are operating in one developing country or another; indeed it would be difficult to find a large company which did not have an overseas division or supplier. They can just establish a project wherever they are. It may require a local partner – why not a woman? – to get it started. Nobody is saying go halfway round the world and do something new in completely unfamiliar territory. Just open your eyes to the potential around you.

Are women actually helping themselves? A fair question to ask, and the answer is that they are where they can. One of the finest and longest-running examples is the SEWA Lucknow chikan embroidery project, based on SEWA Ahmedabad founded by Ella Bhatt in 1972. There are some ten SEWA projects in operation. SEWA means service, but the acronym stands for Self Employed Women's Association. In her book *Embroidering Lives*, Clare Wilkinson-Weber wrote:

> Among the concerns that helped launch the organization were the recognition that women's work was not subsidiary but central, and that women need recognition as workers, moreover as workers who could be organized. SEWA Ahmedabad held that female workers needed special support in the form of healthcare, childcare, skills training, legal aid, reliable work supplies and, in general, assistance in dealing effectively with the public world.

The impact on women's self esteem and confidence as a result of projects like these as I have mentioned is huge. They realise they can contribute more than just toiling away at domestic chores and generate some income as well. This makes an enormous difference to the family, quite disproportionate to the modest additional wage the woman actually generates. In other words, the model works and has been working for nearly 40 years; just imagine what strides could be made with the additional financial firepower and backing of big business.

I would like to quote from a letter I received from Susan Headlam MBE, who lived and worked in Bangladesh for 25 years as Co-Coordinator of a Community Health Programme in Chandraghona in the Rangamati Hill Tracts. She explained how every year she introduced a different programme including clean water, immunisation, adult literacy, but in 1986 she came up with a new idea:

> I decided to introduce an income generating project and we established a weaving factory with a tailoring centre. We chose weaving as it is a declining traditional skill in the area and there was a good market for selling handloom,

100 per cent cotton fabric and readymade garments. Many destitute women gained employment over the years. Not only did they earn money, but they had a better quality of life and a sense of worth. We used to say it was the only place in Bangladesh where women from all religions ate together around one table …

Looking back, the single intervention in the programme which gave the biggest improvement in health was our weaving project giving women an income.

The facts speak for themselves. At a stroke, this single initiative had provided money and improved health, and had even done its bit for inter-religious harmony. It is possible. There are so many private–public partnership funds, but they are not coordinated. Global funds have been found wanting and there are numerous think tanks all working away at their research and producing their reports. I don't want to belittle what they do and the efforts they make at highlighting the plight of the poor, but study their documents, dissect their analysis, and you will be astonished how few paragraphs actually speak about women, and few suggest that women themselves should be helped to take the lead. There are plenty of photographs of babies in their mothers' arms looking plaintively out at the reader; there is talk about growth, about creating the right conditions, about international financial architecture, and there are enough surveys to last many a lifetime. But where are the women? They don't have much left in their lifetime. Every conceivable alternative has been tried but no one, apart from the stalwart likes of SEWA, which spotted the need to focus on women so long ago, has considered trying to help women understand what should be done.

I am tired of seminars listening to people who only want to hear themselves talking. Indian intellectuals I am afraid have got it down to a fine art: the professional conference-goers and seminar-attendees. It looks good on your CV that you have presented a paper at such and such an event, but has it had any impact on the girl looking out in desperation from her slum dwelling clinging to a railway embankment outside New Delhi station?

Strangely enough, I am optimistic that change will come about eventually, in the sense that there is a very slow recognition emerging mainly at the NGO level. In fact there are many wonderful examples of successful NGO efforts with women – Plan International,[28] SEWA and Marie Stopes – including bold sex education courses in places like Bangladesh. Last time I was there I was introduced to a girl who had managed to stop a child marriage. She had stirred up other people in her village and made such a fuss that the wedding was called off.

---

28 Plan International was founded in 1937 and is one of the world's largest development organisations. It raises over US$500 million every year to support its work in 49 developing countries helping all children realise their full potential.

So something is happening, slowly and painstakingly, but not through the most important element in this century, which is global business, and to my mind the leaders of these powerful companies are the ones who must engage for all our sakes. Of course, there will be nervousness in the boardrooms about making an effort to divert activity to women. Men won't like it at first; they will warn that male workers could stage a strike, so why take the risk? The answer is because it could well be profitable. If they want to think altruistically as well, knowing that they would be doing their bit for corporate social responsibility, so much the better, but I would say that is a by-product. I don't want to divert CEOs from running their business in a professional way, but what I would guarantee is that in almost every new project they will have a better and more reliable workforce that will deliver on time. I remember flying back from a trip to Africa, and a fellow passenger told me that her husband's factory had had to close. I asked her if he had employed any women and she said no. I suggested that that was his first mistake. Somebody has to try it and see. You always have to take a risk to find the benefit.

4

THE BLAME GAME

You can't fix a problem without knowing what caused it, so let's ask the blunt question: who is to blame for womankind being reduced to nothing more than an object, a possession, someone valued only for her unpaid labour?

The culture of placing woman second is not just confined to the developing countries. If we go back a century, it was exactly the same in Europe; women have had to fight for their rights in the UK. Every national culture has always treated women in this way. Change can only come about if women feel strong enough to stand up for themselves or when some outside event forces change: in western countries like Britain, this sense of self-worth was attained, or realised, as a result of the two world wars. Women acquired their rights because they were needed in both wars – most did not fight the enemy face to face but their contribution was critical.[29] Now obviously we can't rely on world wars to help the cause of women; in fact the wars that are being fought in Africa are having exactly the opposite effect because women become a convenient target, and they suffer disproportionately as a result of these conflicts. They are not in a position to fight for their rights and, sadly, I have to say there isn't enough willpower or maybe authority among the women who are successful in those countries to bring about the change necessary for others less able or fortunate than they are to fend for themselves. Once they do succeed, women are concerned that if they take up the baton of women's issues they may lose credibility with their male counterparts. Perhaps they should just give it a try, but I am not holding my breath.

A prominent female politician is Tzipi Livni. She was the first woman in Israel to hold the post of foreign minister since Golda Meir in the 1960s. She has since gone on to become the first woman to be leader of the Opposition, heading the Kadima party. But she apparently is very wary of being tied to women's causes. Orit Kamir, a Hebrew University law professor, was quoted in the British press as saying: 'Livni says at every chance she gets that she is not a feminist and has never participated in legislation related to women's issues and because of this she really is free of any feminist imagery.'[30] If women in a society like Israel, where they play a full part, even as soldiers, feel uncertain about being too closely associated with their 'sisters' problems' then Africa and India really do have a long way to go.

There is absolutely no reason why any man in Africa or the sub-continent should want change because it weakens their hold on power and weakens their position as they see it – almost their divine right. That is the way it has always been: man commands, woman obeys. Why would they want women to have more power? On the other hand, it is still possible for women to make a financial contribution to the family without it appearing to be an attack on the very manhood of their husbands or their perceived status, because we have seen this happening with the NGOs who are working daily with women.

It is all too easy to say that this is the way things are done in Africa or India, or indeed Europe. This culture will only change if help comes from an outside source because poor women themselves cannot instigate such change. Unless there is some external trigger, it cannot happen. And there is no more successful, quicker or more benign trigger than helping women to earn small amounts of money. The impact is quite disproportionate to the apparently trivial sums involved.

---

29 In the UK the suffragettes' campaign for the right of women to vote was put on hold during the First World War when women proved they were indispensable working in the fields and munitions factories. The Representation of the People Act, giving women over 30 years the right to vote, was passed in 1918 – ten years later, the age qualification was abolished.

30 Dina Kraft. 'Tzipi Livni: rising star of Israeli politics', *Sunday Telegraph*, 4 January 2009.

Do I believe that it is possible for national culture to change? Yes, without any doubt. National cultures constantly change: that is the nature of culture itself. But unless you introduce an outside element you will never know how much it can change, and few are willing to take the plunge and introduce that element. We can't rely on politicians. No matter what their political persuasion, politicians today are there because they think a lot of themselves, and their key focus is keeping their own seat of power at all costs. The last thing they want to do is disturb their constituents; if they think that by focusing on women they will upset the comfortable and successful status quo then they will never do anything. The 2008/9 national budget in India allocated US$15 billion for social expenditure and the debt relief programme for small farmers – among whom there is a high incidence of suicide – but how much of this sort of money gets to the poor? Every politician in the land knows full well that much of it gets siphoned off along the way, but not one of them is prepared to end the practice because to do so would offend too many people and disturb the comfortable equilibrium of corruption. It seems they would rather have their country held up as a nation where the vast majority are starving and malnourished than lose their perks and kick-backs.

If you look at the legislation on the statute books to protect women, there are more laws in India than in the UK. But if laws are not enforced then there is no point in enacting them. There are clinics in rural areas which are supposed to be manned by a doctor and a nurse. But a survey found that 60 per cent of the time nobody was there because both doctor and nurse were working in the towns earning better money. Or worse, in the more lawless states like Bihar, if a woman goes to the police to complain about some abuse she is just as likely to be raped in the police station itself. It is scarcely believable, but according to the World Health Organization one woman in five around the world, not just in Africa or the sub-continent, is likely to be the victim of rape or attempted rape in her lifetime. Somewhere in America, a woman is raped every two minutes, according to the US Department of Justice, and the FBI estimates that only 37 per cent of cases get reported. So much for the laws: women are not protected and they are not valued. If a person has no value then why would anyone waste any effort on them? This is the battleground on which we have to fight, in countries where laws are either flouted or ignored, sometimes even by the powers that be who should be enforcing them.

Am I being too cynical about politics? I don't think so. Just look how politicians ruthlessly targeted the religious vote in the 2008 American presidential elections. For many years it was the Republicans who had cornered the God vote and won the support of the powerful evangelical movement. Then the Democrats realised there was mileage in faith, and Barack Obama's campaign team began trawling the churches regardless of creed. In his article 'Closing the God Gap',[31] James Crabtree wrote:

> The 'interfaith gathering,' in front of 6000 guests, saw sermons from three Catholics, three rabbis, and a seemingly endless further line-up of imams, Buddhists and Pentecostals. Prayers from prominent pastors began and closed each day's proceedings. Delegates could attend close to a dozen faith-based events, from wonky panel discussions to 'faith caucus' meetings and prayer breakfast. Democrats in Denver seemed born again.

Ultimately, as politicians are the lawmakers, the responsibility must rest with them. I do not have a lot of faith in politicians in Africa or the sub-continent because, like politicians the world over, they have to look after themselves first and foremost. But in the region we are focusing on, where literally lives are at stake on a daily basis, it seems that they are not only reluctant to act in the best interests of women but actually hostile. The appointment of a woman President in India is unconvincing, and I fear only amounts to window dressing. I have far more faith in the NGOs, who have proved time and again that women can be organised as a labour force. They can earn money and can change their own lives for the better and those of their families. In Africa and the sub-continent there are now some businesses that are taking their corporate responsibilities seriously. Standard Chartered Bank has long been involved in combating Aids and began running its own 'Living with HIV' programme in its workplaces in 2003. In fact the bank says that volunteer staff members educate other employees and raise awareness about HIV across 50 countries in which it operates.

So it is happening, but for most it is not the thing to do; it is just an adjunct to apparently more pressing matters. What is required is for business to see that women are available for work just as readily as they would think of men being available for work. If they are worried that a woman can't be employed because she has children, or is likely to have children, then give her a part-time job. Two women can share the work. Ultimately it is a question of changing the mindset. A woman is a person, not something hidden behind a man, and the reality is that she is actually keeping the world going by selflessly undertaking all the tasks that get no reward or thanks. It is as though she has no meaning or relevance beyond the purely domestic person, a non-being.

When I was in Jamaica I noticed that the women, as usual, were doing much of the unrecognised work. They were not in positions of power but they certainly kept the country on track. I was talking to a secretary to the Parliament, fulfilling an important but typically invisible role – she had no status. I asked her how quickly

---

31   James Crabtree. 'Closing the God Gap', Issue 137, *Prospect*, 25 October 2008.

she thought the country would come to a standstill if women went on strike for a day and only looked after babies and sick people. I think we both realised that it would be no more than a matter of hours.

It was both tragic and informative when the tsunami struck Aceh in Indonesia on Boxing Day 2004. Among the TV stories were the images of some unfortunate man who was saying his wife had died and he didn't know what to do. He was asking who was going to cook his food now. It seemed to sum up just how dependent men can be for every little thing in their lives – the wretched man was more concerned about his next meal than the loss of his wife. It might even help the men if they became more self-sufficient in their own domestic lives.

I have never hidden my disdain for much of what religion professes to be doing in the name of humanity – in the name of man, perhaps; woman never. The question is do I believe that religion is helping or hindering. If you believe that religion is created by man rather than God then it starts to make sense – and I don't mean man in the collective sense. All the major religions of the world are male-centred. There is no doubt about that. Even if the founders had good things to say about women and showed respect for them, those thoughts have disappeared like dimly remembered folklore, and all kinds of taboos and treatments have developed which you cannot find in the original founders' words or views. How is it that through the centuries the Catholic Church has robbed the poor to become rich? I supposed it robbed the rich as well. Everyone had to pay tithes to the Church. The Church made sure there were serfs and kept them in serfdom. But did Jesus Christ say to do that? Absolutely not. He taught the very opposite, and yet we have this in the Catholic Church today which professes to be the only true faith. Women are only respected in the form of Mary, who did not give birth in the normal way but was said to be impregnated by God. What does this do for an ordinary woman? She is not impregnated by God but by her husband, or she is raped, so she is not chaste and not to be respected in the sense that Mary is. The Church does not identify everyday women with Mary, but it should. Women bring new life into the world and they should be respected for that alone. It is an insult to all womankind not to acknowledge the significance of this primary function.

The gurus of the Swaminarayan sect, a sect based on Hinduism, founded at the end of the 18th century in northern India, will not allow women into their presence. This stems from the teaching of the founder, Lord Shree Swaminarayan – who while condemning such practices as the act of *sati* (the killing of a widow on her husband's funeral pyre) and *doodh piti* (the drowning of a newly born daughter in milk), and promoting the education of women – established separate orders for ascetic men and women so that religious teaching could be given without them having to meet the opposite sex. I was not popular when I advised the Royal Household at the time of the Queen's Jubilee that Her Majesty should not visit their London headquarters, Neasden Temple, in case she was snubbed by not being introduced to the head of their faith in the UK. What could possibly be wrong with meeting a woman? They seem to forget that they too were born of a woman.

Any discussion about the role of religion in poorer countries very swiftly moves to the issue of family planning. In the early days it might have been a good idea to have as many children as possible. Life expectancy could be short and many hands were needed to work the land. But it has long ceased to be a good idea. If we are to save this planet we have to have fewer people, but nobody is willing to talk about it. All the environmentalists talk about is recycling and not flying, or conserving water, electricity and the rainforest; but what about the growing population? No amount of recycling is going to save the planet if we don't start trying to control the population increase. The problem, as Boris Johnson, who became Mayor of London, wrote in October 2007,[32] is that we can no longer discuss fertility and the population explosion without someone taking offence. He wrote: 'we are getting to the point where you simply can't discuss [the fertility of the human race], and we are thereby refusing to say anything sensible about the biggest single challenge facing the Earth; and no, whatever it may now be conventional to say, the single biggest challenge is not global warming. That is a secondary challenge. The primary challenge facing our species is the reproduction of our species itself.'

I know that the Catholic Church is against abortion, and that I can understand; there are many people against abortion, but if you don't have family planning then you are likely to have more need of abortion. I would say to an anti-abortionist: when a woman wants to have an abortion, why don't you promise that you will help her to keep that baby and pay for its upbringing, instead of shouting at her? No anti-abortionist yet has offered to help keep and bring up a baby for a mother, no matter how dire her problems. They just say you can't have an abortion. If they do offer to support the child then I will be all in favour of the anti-abortionists. Criticism and guilt are not going to help a desperate woman. If the Catholic Church believed in and promoted some form of family planning other than the impossible option of abstinence there would be an immediate change because it is the poorest and least educated who are the most easily manipulated and have the most difficulty in bringing up and educating their children.

The Catholic Church is a great barrier in this matter, although it is interesting to note that the fertility rate of Italy has gone down to 1.2 children per couple –

32   Boris Johnson. 'Global over-population is the real issue', *Daily Telegraph*, 25 October 2007.

among the lowest in the world; clearly either they have got a magic formula which they haven't shared with the rest of us, or the Pope has no influence over his own flock in the Vatican. But while the population trend in Europe may be declining, among the poorest people around the world it is increasing, and they are precisely the people who still hear the Catholic message and practise the rhythm method of family planning, because they feel they are committing a sin if they use any other method.

There is a difference between the religions. I take no issue with the Anglicans. The Sikhs are meant to treat their women as equals, but what a religion teaches and what its followers practise are not always the same. Hindus do not always treat women well and some Muslim men treat them even worse, contrary to the teachings of the Qur'an. There are many verses in the Qur'an that can be interpreted in different ways, and it seems to me that the current interpretation is all on the side of being anti-women's rights instead of moving forward. I know that this very statement could be met with a flurry of quotations from the Qur'an suggesting the contrary. All I would say is that I can only judge from what I see with my own eyes. I recently watched a television programme about Cairo in the seventies which compared it with scenes today. The difference was striking. In the seventies the women were walking around as in any other part of the world: men and women going about their business, mixing together. Now there are fewer women on the streets; most have some sort of scarf and some are completely covered up. The Egyptian women were among the best educated in the seventies; they were lawyers and teachers, and people used to go to Egyptian colleges and universities that were world-renowned.

What is happening now? It seems Islam is looking back to the eighth century instead of moving towards being a part of the modern world. The cruelty towards women manifested in such forms as honour killings compounded by the defence of these and other atrocities is horrendous. It is neither honourable nor religious. Religion could be a force for good and help change society, but the people who are running the religions – priests, preachers and imams – are all men. It would not suit them to bring about change. In his last sermon the Prophet Muhammad said: 'Treat your women well and be kind to them for they are your partners and committed helpers.' No one could argue with that sentiment, but why is it not practised more openly? Of course, in Islam, just as in many religions, there are differences and I should not generalise. There are radicals and traditionalists, liberals and zealots, and in Islam there has been division ever since the death of the Prophet Muhammad as to who are the true followers of the faith: there is tension between Arab and non-Arab Islam, there are the Sunnis and the Shias, the result of a ferocious leadership struggle within 20 years of the Prophet Muhammad's death.

I have no wish to attack Islam, but we must be able to say that not all practitioners of the faith are spotless. Patrick Sookhdeo, the eminent academic and Director of the Institute for the Study of Islam and Christianity, warned British politicians against accepting 'the view of British Islam as an ideal society of peace, tolerance and moral values'. He said: 'The reality, however, includes a rather different aspect. High crime rates, street gangs, oppression of women and radicalisation leading to terrorist violence seem equally to characterise the community and reveal the deep problems and rifts within it. Ignoring such problems will only exacerbate them rather than help eradicate them.'[33]

What one might call moderate and right thinking Muslims say is that the abusive treatment meted out to women is not in the Qur'an, but why don't they stand up against it? They argue that these are only isolated incidents, but even so, why not condemn them? Surely what the Taliban tried to impose in Afghanistan between 1996 and 2001 had nothing to do with Islam. People don't have to protest publicly if they fear for their lives, but why is there no powerful Islamic movement in the West against the extremists who seem to be taking over the moderate interpretation of the faith; why don't they protest that to abuse women contravenes Islamic teaching? None of us believes that you should treat women worse than an animal, but it sometimes seems that an animal has more value than a woman. The Prophet Muhammad tried to change all that, because women were bought and sold as nothing more than possessions in pre-Islamic Arabia. They were worth less than a camel – more than a goat, but less than a camel – so why is Islam allowing this, we have to ask. What would the Prophet think if he were alive today?

The reason why no one speaks up is undoubtedly fear. But the way to combat abuse is perfectly simple: all Muslims should start treating their own women better. They don't have to say anything publicly: if they just do it at home the effect will spread. Instead we are going backwards: in Egypt there were highly educated women in every profession and now their numbers are fewer.

Confusion and contradiction seem to abound in religious practice. The Anglicans, for example, are at sixes and sevens over what to do about women priests. How can a woman be allowed to become a priest and then not rise to the top (bishop or even archbishop)? The role of women is just as likely to cause a schism as the marriage between homosexuals or – horror of horrors – between gay clergy members. Blocking the career path of women in the church is not a decision based on merit but one based purely on gender and prejudice. Why make them priests in the first place? What exists at the moment is a second-class group of clerics – women priests. They

---

33   Patrick Sookhdeo. *Faith, Power and Territory: A Handbook of British Islam*, Isaac Publishing, 2008.

can conduct all the ceremonies, deliver the sermons and expect their preaching to be believed, but they can never reach the highest echelons in the Anglican Communion because of their gender. It is a boys-own club, and the old guard believe that women should never have been allowed to join in the first place. It is a complete giveaway. In my opinion, it is bound to lead to a split in the church sooner or later and a weakening of its position

So we have members of a single religion who don't agree, and different faiths who each believe that only they are blessed with the divine knowledge. They can't all be right, and surely if there is a god there can only be one. Before Christianity, Judaism or Islam claim that they have first rights, don't forget Zoroastrianism, once the state religion of Persia, was teaching belief in one God, good and evil, heaven and hell, a thousand years before the Arabs even reached Persia. You can't create a different god for different colours. If only religion had been favourable to women, or even if it had treated men and women equally, the world would have been very different today. Religion has a lot to answer for in the inequality of women, and while it may speak of the value and importance of women this counts for little if they are segregated and have to receive their instruction carefully separated from men.

One would like to think that impartial organisations like the United Nations could deliver the solution. With great enthusiasm they launched the Decade of Women to run from 1976 to 1985, with the first world conference held in Mexico City. There was a ten-point agenda but it didn't get anywhere. In her speech at a gathering in Nairobi marking the end of the Decade, Leticia R. Shahani, Secretary General of the World Conference, said: 'The Decade has caused the invisible majority of humankind – the women – to be more visible on the global scene.' I am not convinced. The reality is that the Decade of Women, which had the backing of representatives from more than 150 countries and some 263 NGOs, had no impact on the lives of impoverished women around the globe. The key achievement was said to be the recognition of the essential role of women in development. If it was recognised by governments, little of substance has emerged in practice. Indeed no sooner had the Cairo conference reached some form of consensus on a 20-year Programme of Action to try to put women's equality, empowerment, reproductive rights and sexual health at the centre of population and development policies, than it was being undermined by the Vatican, some conservative Islamic countries and several Latin American states, who were staunchly opposed to provisions about reproductive health and reproductive rights. Now we have got the Millennium Development Goals, which are said to be women-centred. They cannot possibly meet a tenth of their targets precisely because there is no specific focus on women; if there were then undoubtedly we would at least make some progress towards reaching those Goals.

Some years ago I was at a lecture by the then Secretary General of the UN, Kofi Annan, at the Commonwealth Institute. I suggested that for the next five years we should give all development aid to help poor women. The whole of the conference hall applauded. Kofi Annan said in reply that a great deal was already being done for women – in other words, he just fudged the issue. So I don't have much faith in mighty organisations like the UN to help either.

Deep down I actually believe that men just don't understand. I am not sure that many African men or Indian men have any real feeling for women. I think they see women in two ways: one, they are relatives; or two, they are someone to flirt with. I don't know how they actually perceive women in general. And poor women don't come into their psychology at all; they don't exist. There is an organisation called Vidya, started by my friend Rashmi Misra, that teaches slum children. One day we were at dinner at the British High Commission in Delhi, sitting at the table with the country's Permanent Secretary from the Home Ministry. My friend said that we can deal with everything; we can deal with the children and we can deal with the women, who are delighted with everything we do for them. The problem, she said, was the men, and the Permanent Secretary started laughing. I asked him why he considered these matters so amusing. I don't think men feel any guilt; if they did they would do something about it. I don't think the Permanent Secretary himself felt any guilt or even understood the significance of what was being said.

While I would never point the finger of blame at charities, I would like to know whether anyone has done an audit to see where all the money raised has gone, who has been helped, how much has been sent to whom. We hear of the big *tamashas*, the great concerts, but who has been saved, how many and in which country? If the poor are getting poorer, which they are in greater numbers, and more and more charity donations are made every year, clearly something does not add up. Now it is fair to say that it is not up to charities to try to change the culture of a country, but there is something of the little boy sticking his finger in the dam to stop the leak about so much charitable work. All it would take is a little redirection and refocus.

Having said that, there is some heroic work being done by NGOs; if only they and other charities could convert all the money that is donated into something directly applicable to women they would see an enormous benefit to the communities they are helping. The big five charities could certainly focus more on women. They have become like government departments, and they are very powerful; if they are doing something specific for women then we are not hearing about it.

This is not a case of asking charities to interfere with the normal running of a country – they are after all supposed to be apolitical, but it would not threaten any government if they could, for example, help women establish cooperatives. Everyone would benefit. I would accept man remaining king for the time being, but at least allow woman to be queen with some sense of dignity and a rightful and recognised position in the community. Men will only feel threatened if they feel insecure, and they will only feel insecure if they know they have been unjust.

I will look at how women treat each other in more detail in the next chapter, but on the subject of blame I believe women have been, and still are, too compliant. The reason is partly that they don't know any other way – that is the nature of their life and they accept it. In India they would put it down to their bad *karma*. They cannot imagine any alternative. They get up before the men, prepare the food and make everything ready for the men to go off to the fields. They are at work all day, caring for the children, looking after the animals and helping in the fields as well; they are up first and go to bed last.

You might ask how, if they are so busy, they will find time to work in the new 'business model' I am proposing. The answer is that if there is paid work they will find the time to do it. If there is some embroidery they will do it at home. They will get other women to look after the children. It is not that they can't find the time, but that their time could be better spent; for example, improvements could be made to their daily lives by bringing water to the village via a pump instead of them spending hours and, quite literally in war-torn Africa, risking their lives to carry a jar of water back to their homes. There is pioneering work being done by the likes of Faith Singh and her ANOKHI company in Jaipur; she brings in girls and women and trains them to work in her clothing factory. The impact is enormous, because normally these girls would never even be allowed to think of working outside their homes.

My sincere hope is that by gaining some education girls in India and Africa will learn that they don't have to accept 'their lot'; they can fight for a better life and then use their knowledge and experience to change the lives of their families. This sort of empowerment is naturally something some religions and some men would want to prevent them acquiring. There can be no other reason for holding women back. If you are constantly told you are worthless and your only purpose in life is to look after your husband and your in-laws, you either come to believe that it is true and remain compliant, or you try to find an alternative purpose to your life.

Nor should I point the finger of blame at businesses. There are many that have done a great deal of good for the communities in which they operate. There is no law that says they should do even that, although to my way of thinking it makes sound business sense to support your neighbourhood. However, while I place no blame on businesses, they now have to sit up, look to the future and understand where their business model needs to change. If we are to save humanity and the environment, and all businesses share some responsibility in this regard, they have to look at the status of women in their business cycle, because only women can bring about real change.

Picking up on the Chinese proverb 'Women hold up half the sky', Lloyd Blankfein, the chairman of Goldman Sachs, launched the Wall Street bank's own private initiative focused exclusively on women in developing countries. In 2008 he announced that the bank would spend $100 million over five years to help 10,000 women to improve their managerial and entrepreneurial education. The focus is to be on practical skills, not theory. In Goldman's own economic research report it stated that gender equality has a 'key role to play as a source of support for long-term economic growth. Bringing more women into the labor force could provide a substantial boost to GDP growth and per capita income.' The report continued: 'Arguably there may be no better investment for the health and development of poor countries around the world than investments to educate children.'[34]

I believe that this century is the century of global businesses, and it is time for them to take their rightful place in helping the planet and not think they can do that by changing the light bulbs or reducing their carbon footprint. Businesses must consider the major change required by helping women look after the health of their families, teaching them to have fewer children, making sure men use condoms and teaching them to look after their own environment. They can do all this by the simple expedient of giving women a small role in their organisations. If women can actually believe that they have the capacity to contribute and achieve all these things, they will move the proverbial mountain. The solution costs so little: just a few pennies to give them some independence. They mustn't duck the issue by saying the use of condoms is nothing to do with them, or that what a husband and wife do at home is not their concern. It is their concern. We are all on the same planet. We are not going to be exempt from the impact that a growing population in India or Africa will have on global warming. We need to be together working to this end and, as we have seen, it cannot be left to the politicians or national leaders. They can be blamed for the failure so far but, having identified the culprits, it is time to restore order.

There is only one miracle possible. There is nothing else coming round the corner. But we just do not wish to recognise the miracle for what it is. Every time an opportunity has been given to women they have grabbed it and run with it, and things have changed in their town or village. So much has been achieved in large areas of India through SEWA, and things have changed in Latin America through Plan's work. In short, life changes wherever women are engaged, and if businesses can embrace this concept then a major global impact will be achieved. All it requires

---

34   Goldman Sachs Global Economics Paper No. 164.

is for businesses to look at their basic structure and add one other component into their thinking: ask themselves where they can use women as a workforce. Why don't they let women run the canteen, stitch the uniforms, set up some small spin-off operation, all the time remembering that the profit reverts back to the company? Unless businesses start looking at their own operations to see what they can do, they will not do anything. I outline specific steps that can be taken later in the book (Chapter 10), but essentially if management started on a small scale it would begin to snowball. It is my hope that if the senior management in businesses opened their minds to this proposal they might find they have a very worthwhile workforce. It may just be a biased opinion, but I think person for person women are faster learners than men; they are much more able to multi-task because they have to do many things simultaneously at home.

If I have a criticism of business it is only that it has not lifted its eyes up from its work to see the opportunity. Doing nothing about solving a global crisis now is no longer an option for the future. There will be more and more people to feed as the population expands by two billion or more by 2050. What have we got to look forward to? What is in store for all of us? The rich may be able to go on living well – but how are we going to bring about a change in the poorest countries? We certainly cannot rely on the financial markets to bail us out after the 2008 financial meltdown, so it is back to basics, a return to the practicalities of life, and that is the very thing that women have been getting on with since time immemorial.

To be fair to businessmen, I don't think they have been dodging the issue; they just cannot understand what I can understand or feel what I can feel. Possibly it is because I am a woman, but also because I have seen what can be done by women. Sometimes, of course, they can see and understand everything and they tremble at the prospect that perhaps women might be able to do things better. I didn't see many female chief executives in all those banks which collapsed around the world. Men don't see women as players, let alone key players – although it was remarkable that on 20 October 2008, just days after the 'meltdown', the leaders of some of the UK's top companies wrote an open letter to the *Daily Telegraph* saying there was an urgent need to get more women into senior positions in British business. The paper also reported that Nadereh Chamlou, a senior adviser at the World Bank, told an international women's forum in France: 'The current economic and financial crisis gives us the opportunity to insert gender into the re-writing of the rules.' It seems that even this cloud may have a silver lining if the call for such a change is realised.

My focus is on persuading men that women are more than capable of handling any task you throw at them. I am not looking at taking over companies or even running countries, I am concentrating on a much bigger agenda: the poorest women.

I am not even searching for equality; I am looking for poverty alleviation, health improvement, the ability for women to control their own fertility and a reduction of serious diseases like Aids. Women can achieve all that if they just have a chance to show their worth for your business.

So this then is my problem: everyone – government, charities, businesses, men and women – shares a collective responsibility. All I am asking is that they each give it a try and be prepared to think laterally, courageously even. If it fails, it will have cost virtually nothing; it will require no multi-billion dollar bail-out if a few canteens or a small farming cooperative fail, and if they do I shall eat humble pie. But no one is willing to try, and they are not willing because they fear it is going to upset the whole order of things. Well, you don't get miracles without upsetting the order of things, and I am not calling for a revolution. Change can also be achieved little by little.

Men behave the way they are expected to behave and, regrettably at times, women behave the way they are expected to behave. You have got to break that system, that mindset; everybody has to work together to break it, and as businesses are now so powerful, we look to them to help. If the approach is business-driven then it becomes something which is not only sustainable but is self-sustaining.

There is one question that needs to be asked whenever a new initiative is being considered in the boardrooms, particularly in Africa and the sub-continent: what and where is the role for women in your organisation?

Let me close this chapter by quoting from the success of Tata Steel's initiative in 2002 to do the unthinkable and train women to drive heavy machinery at a plant in India:

> Tata Steel's Tejaswini project is a remarkable empowerment initiative that has seen 23 ordinary women become operators and drivers of heavy-duty machinery and vehicles.
>
> Perched on her forklift truck moving heavy materials, Sunaina Devi is a proud tejaswini, which roughly translates into 'woman who shines like a beacon'. A clearer definition of this mother of a 22-year-old son is that she's a role model for others of her gender. It has taken a while, but Sunaina finally feels that she is doing something worthwhile with her life.
>
> Asha Hansda is a chip off the same block. She bicycles to work all the way from her village, then muscles up to operating a bulldozer and a 35-tonne dumper truck. 'I have a prestigious job,' she says. 'When I operate the bull-dozer at the waste recycling plant, sitting 8 feet high, I feel like I'm on top of the world. I also drive the heaviest dumper, which makes me a unique metal girl.'
>
> The enthusiasm and conviction of these tejaswinis is infectious. Self-belief shines through the eyes, words and demeanour of Ms Sunaina, Ms Asha and

others like them. From being rejas (female counterparts of mazdoor, or labourers) to becoming tejaswinis with Tata Steel at Jamshedpur, theirs has been a fairytale transformation.

These are women from the grassroots who worked as 'attendants' and 'office girls', never hoping to go beyond cleaning and serving tea for the rest of their lives. Then, as part of the Tata Steel women's empowerment plan, with a little encouragement and training, they blossomed to reveal their actual abilities. Project Tejaswini was conceived and launched in 2002 to provide women employees at Tata Steel with a platform to unleash their potential. What began as an experiment has turned out to be a huge success; the tejaswinis are now considered as good, if not better, mobile equipment drivers as their male counterparts.

Laxmi Kumari is another of these proud tejaswinis. Brimming with self-worth and satisfaction, she says: 'When my neighbours address me as driver sahiba instead of chaiwali, my heart swells with pride. In the past I have been someone's wife, mother or daughter. Now I am my own person. I have a purpose in life.'

The seeds of the project were sown when Niroop Mahanty, vice president (HR), RBB Singh, president of the Tata Steel workers' union, and BN Sarangi, chief HR/IR (steel), had an informal discussion about how to give growth opportunities to the women employees of Tata Steel. Instead of looking only at avenues in 'women's work', why not nurture and groom a few talented female employees to operate heavy mobile equipment like their male colleagues? In September 2002, vacancies were announced and application forms invited. The selection process assessed the women's will power, physical strength and their spirit of adventure. After a rigorous selection process, 13 women were selected from the 40 who had applied. Their transformation process began on November 3, 2002.

There was apprehension among workers, management and trainees alike. Some thought it a waste of money while others reckoned it was too daunting a job for women. The women themselves were a bundle of nerves, despite their enthusiasm. Mental, physical and social barriers had to be crossed – each step was a challenge. Learning to handle the huge equipment was the ultimate challenge, but changing from a sari to trousers and a shirt was the immediate one. During the driving lessons, while some hesitated even to mount the monstrous machines, others couldn't wait to drive them around.

Apart from being trained to operate the equipment, the tejaswinis were also imparted basic knowledge of their technical aspects, so as to enable them to appreciate their jobs better. Sessions on motivation and confidence building were part of the three-month training programme, designed by project coordinator Urmila Ekka with the help of equipment maintenance head PK Singh and equipment maintenance manager Sanjay Kumar. Mr Kumar imparted detailed training on the finer aspects of the various kinds of machinery: bulldozers, mechanical shovels, dumpers, tractors, forklifts of various capacities, light commercial vehicles, etc.

The technical inputs included an introduction of all types of vehicles, making a preliminary inspection before starting the vehicle, an overview of different types of diesel vehicles and their major sub-systems like fuel, steering, brake, lubrication, cooling and exhaust air systems, power transmission systems, an introduction to hydraulic systems, functioning of hydraulic pumps, hydraulic cylinders and control valves.

Trained drivers Ranvijay Singh and Sushil Kumar taught the women the actual operation of the heavy mobile equipment. During their hands-on training, not a single woman met with an accident, which boosted their confidence and helped them achieve their goal. Says Ranvijay Singh: 'The trainees picked up very well from the third day onwards. They were full of enthusiasm and determination.'

The women were also briefed on the steel manufacturing process, quality circles, dealing with customers, interpersonal skills, positive thinking, fire fighting, team building and road traffic rules. Mr Sarangi also arranged for visits from successful women to motivate them. Bachendri Pal, head of the Tata Steel Adventure Foundation and the first Indian woman to climb Mount Everest, gave tips on leadership skills and encouraged them to reach for the stars. Rupa Mahanty, a successful management consultant, conducted motivation sessions.

Three months of training transformed the simple rejas into efficient tejaswinis. There was support from family members, the Tata Steel management and the union. On January 3, 2003, when the 13 tejaswinis first publicly displayed their prowess on the heavy vehicles, they ushered in a new era in the history of Tata Steel, even as they embarked on a new life for themselves.

Interestingly, the first batch of 13 women holds a record for accident-free driving since they began work 21 months ago. In April 2004, another batch of 10 tejaswinis was trained and commissioned as mobile heavy equipment drivers. Aged between 33 and 42 years, the new tejaswinis are successfully operating huge cranes, rigging machines, welding machines, gas cutters and other precision instruments.

For all 23, it is not just the self-image of the woman that has undergone a transformation — their everyday lives and that of their families has changed forever. They are now financially sound, earning about Rs 10,000 a month as junior operators, which is more than double what they made earlier. If they maintain their commitment, precision and enthusiasm at work, they could well move up the ladder, become senior operators and take home as much as Rs 23,000 a month before they retire.

It has been a kind of revolution in itself, not just for these women but also for Tata Steel; in the 96 years of its history, women had never before done a man's job.

5

WOMEN VERSUS WOMEN AND OTHER FORMS OF VIOLENCE

It is always so easy to accuse others when often the fault lies much closer to home. When I first went to the House of Lords in 1990 I found it to be quite reserved, and it took me some months to start making friends. Then I realised that the people who appeared reserved were just shy and it was a question of first breaking down that barrier of shyness.

As I learned more about the so-called boys in the House of Lords, I began to notice how much they looked after each other. I found that if there was somebody in trouble, with either health or money problems, they would rally round and find some way of helping that person; they would try to organise a solution to their money worries, or if someone was in hospital they would arrange visits. I was very impressed by their solidarity. This was at the time of hereditary peers, to whom I am referring. What intrigued me was that they weren't competitive

with each other. They were supportive, especially in times of trouble. I eventually asked a fellow peer how it was that they were so good at looking after each other while women seemed less inclined to back one another up. He said they had been doing it for 2,000 years while we women had just started; we had got to give ourselves some time. A 2,000 year old boys' club – I was very struck by that.

In my experience women don't have such a strong fellow feeling towards one another. I find that if you are on a committee, for example, then the women compete with each other. They want to show up the other women. I am sorry to say women are not sisters as they like to believe – there is no question about it. For example, if a man is disabled women will rush up to him and ask how he is, but if a woman is disabled women will still go up to the husband and ask how he is managing; I should know, since my husband has been disabled for over 20 years. I pointed this curious phenomenon out when I spoke at the Albert Hall to a gathering of the Townswomen's Guild and asked the audience who they thought women went to when a woman was in a wheelchair, and they all shouted from the floor: 'The man!'

This, of course, is all so far removed from the poverty of Africa and the Indian sub-continent we are addressing, but if instinctively, even in the so-called developed world, women are not treating each other as sisters and people to be supported, then what hope is there for the rest of the world who have so much less?

Who is it who dishes the dirt and maltreats the daughters-in-law in the Indian households? The mothers-in-law, of course. The son can do no wrong, and in return the son still idolises his mother. Who carries out the female genital mutilation (FGM) on young girls in Africa? It is all practised by the women. FGM – the partial or total removal of the external female genitalia, or other injury to the female genital organs for non-medical reasons – is so destructive to a woman; she cannot enjoy any sexual pleasure in life and the result is that she cannot have any normal sex life because she is in pain all the time. The basic facts from the World Health Organization make appalling reading but need to be understood. It is most common in Africa, where it is estimated that 92 million girls aged ten and over have undergone FGM, but also in Asia and the Middle East. It continues among immigrants to North America and Europe. Even when you try to stop it happening and laws are passed, it is difficult to take action.

WHO key facts:

- Female genital mutilation (FGM) includes procedures that intentionally alter or injure female genital organs for non-medical reasons.

- An estimated 100 to 140 million girls and women worldwide are currently living with the consequences of FGM.

- In Africa, about three million girls are at risk of FGM annually.

- The procedure has no health benefits for girls and women.

- Procedures can cause severe bleeding and problems urinating, and later, potential childbirth complications and newborn deaths.

- It is mostly carried out on young girls sometime between infancy and age 15 years.

- FGM is internationally recognised as a violation of the human rights of girls and women. [35]

There is envy and a great deal of rivalry among women. The older women resent the younger women working, and this is true in the West as well. It is as if they are saying: 'I didn't get the opportunity to work so why should you?' They see each other as opponents in life's battles rather than as fellow sufferers who should be supported. Of course, this is a generalisation, and obviously all women are not like that, but in the regions we are focusing on it is commonplace. In the West women use their beauty, their guile and wit to stand out from the female competition; in the underdeveloped parts of the world they practise a different cruelty on each other, a physical cruelty. Often that cruelty can be hidden cruelty, mental as well as physical, behind closed doors. If women supported each other that would make a huge difference. It is all about retaining power. Mothers-in-law have the power to mistreat their daughters-in-law, although the power of the mother in the home depends very much on the individual. Some are very strong, some are very clever, and their cleverness is appreciated by the family so they do become the rock around which the family revolves.

The challenge and hope is that when women achieve positions of authority beyond the family, perhaps in local or even national politics where they can do something to espouse women's causes, they will take up that challenge. Unfortunately all too often, if they do speak up they are written off by the mainstream as just being interested in women's rights. I am not naive; it would have been a long hard struggle to reach such status. It is not an easy life for women politicians who have achieved high positions, and they are reluctant to do anything that might threaten their progress.

While we may read of the horrors of honour killings and dowry deaths which are actually carried out by the men, make no mistake that women have been known to trick their daughters-in-law into revealing where they are hiding, pretending to be sympathetic to the cruelty the girl has suffered at the hands of their son. They are even prepared to 'expose' their own daughters, and apparently to stand back when

---

35 World Health Organization.

they too are dragged away. So be in no doubt that women can make the lives of other women totally miserable. Yes, there are wonderful grandmothers who care for their grandchildren – in Africa, there may be no one else if both parents have died from Aids – and quite obviously there are caring mothers-in-law, but the petty cruelties of the boardroom are just as unforgivable as the more physical and mental suffering in a hut in Africa. The onus is on all women to start supporting and stop harming one another. A mother-in-law should not worry about losing control of the household, the rising female politicians should not forget the battles they fought to achieve stardom: only then will we see real change begin to happen.

It is impossible to empower women without a discussion of the sex lives of men and women in Africa and the Indian sub-continent. The United Nations Population Fund said: 'The ability of women to control their own fertility is absolutely fundamental to women's empowerment and equality.' Women are not in control of their fertility, their bodies or their health. We just have to think of all the monogamous women who have HIV in India and are not allowed to go to the clinics because then everyone will know they have been infected by their husbands.

Women often do not get medical help, and one can see the stages of different kinds of illness which would never be seen in the West because it would never be allowed to get to that point. Medicine costs money, and women are not the bread winners, so it is always the man who needs to be looked after, not the woman.

I would like to quote at length from the story of a girl called Narita, who lives in Nepal but could easily have been living in Africa or India. It is a story reported by the White Ribbon Alliance, which promotes safe motherhood. [36] She says:

> Three days after the delivery of my first child, my mother-in-law made me pound the Dhiki [a traditional rice-pounding device made from a block of wood]. While I was working, I felt a severe pain in my lower abdomen and started to bleed heavily.
>
> I went to my mother-in-law and told her about it. She told me that there was no need to worry. But my bleeding did not stop. She continued to force me to collect fodder for the cattle every day.
>
> While lifting the bundle of fodder, I experienced an excruciating pain in my lower abdomen, followed by heavy bleeding. I felt as if I had fallen from a tree. I managed to get home carrying the fodder on my back. On my way home, I told my husband about this problem but he showed no concern. My in-laws also turned a deaf ear while I was writhing in pain. My husband would yell at me and order me to shut up, and so did my in-laws.
>
> Due to the pain, I refused to have intercourse with my husband but he forced me into it because he wanted a child. I would feel extreme pain during

---

36 The White Ribbon Alliance is an international coalition of organisations and individuals in nearly 100 countries which works to save the lives of pregnant women and newborn children around the world.

intercourse and bleed profusely. I noticed part of my abdomen had slipped out of place, but did not know how. When my husband came to know about it, he was not moved by my plight. Instead he threatened to re-marry. My father-in-law even refused to eat the food I cooked.

My in-laws supported my husband and together, they forced me out of the house one day. With great difficulty, I have managed to survive till now. Even the villagers hated me and used abusive language when I passed by.

Cast out by my husband and in-laws, I suffered alone. Often, I felt like committing suicide. In the meantime, as if to rub salt on my wound, I had a second child. After that the pain and bleeding worsened.

A kind lady in the village seeing my condition took me to a woman who handled such cases. Then I came to know that I was suffering from a uterine prolapse. This had happened as a result of heavy work I was made to do right after the child deliveries. She advised me to go to Kohalpur, a town which was a twelve-hour walk away.

In December 2007, I went to Kohalpur all alone and without help from my husband's family. A local NGO helped me, and I was lucky that I survived after an operation. My condition has since improved.

I am telling my story because it can generate awareness among the countless poor women who undergo the same tribulations and ordeals as I did. In the eight wards of the Jajarkot District alone, there could be more than 12,000 women suffering from this problem and yet still deprived of any treatment.'

If you cannot expect support from your own family, what hope is there for so many of these young women? The fact of life in Africa and India is that a woman is replaceable. Every day there are stories such as Narita's or the one I read about a girl of 12 who was sold for two goats. Inevitably, having given birth at such a young age she develops fistula and she will be thrown out by her husband who no longer wants her because she is incontinent. He certainly doesn't mind if she dies – he can always buy another one for a couple more goats. If a woman is so utterly replaceable, like a worn-out shoe, she can be treated just the same.

I cannot understand why fertility and childbirth is only now an issue for the UN. It is such an obvious problem, and one that has been a cause for concern for decades – centuries. If you cannot control your own fertility or you cannot stop having more children because you are under the complete control of the man in your life, who is going to impregnate you whether you are willing or not, then what kind of future can you have? If you do not have any option in the number of children you bear then you cannot even start to have a life of your own.

Maybe now, finally, the world is recognising that women make up half the population, and that perhaps they have something to contribute. I am utterly convinced that if women start earning money it will give them a sense of their own self-worth, which in time will lead to them being interested in controlling their own fertility. Most of these women don't even know that they can, that there are ways of not having so many children. And in my experience, when they know they can stop having more children most women stop in order to give a better life to their existing family. The link between the ability to earn as a result of very basic literacy and fertility is undeniable and is interestingly confirmed in Uganda. The total fertility rate is 7.8 among women with no education and 7.3 among women with some primary education. And when women have more than primary education, the rate dropped to 3.9 in 2000.[37]

There is still some idea that if you have a large family the children will look after you, but if you are in good health, working and have three healthy children instead of six unhealthy children, surely you are going to be better off. You yourself are going to be in a much better state of health; so are your husband and your children. All that comes from having some money. How can you lose? Having fewer children doesn't spoil your future: it improves your future and that of your children. You educate them, you feed them, and it gives you the freedom to do the things you could not do if you had too many. All this seems so obvious that it scarcely needs to be said; and yet, if that were the case, why is there no concerted effort by governments and businesses to bring it about? If those in the affluent West do not have more than one or two children, who then get sent to private schools, surely it is right to help all women to have smaller families, to help them understand the significance of having children and the impact that would have on their lives.

In some rural communities it can be as basic as explaining those elementary details. The impact for the entire world is so clear. We are not talking about billions of dollars of investment and in return world population numbers will slow and eventually may even fall. I don't believe we have a choice in the matter. Our grandchildren may soon be living in a world where even water, if available, is restricted. If the population of Africa alone is going to increase by 1.3 billion, how are they going to be fed and watered?

I asked a doctor why fertility was so high among undernourished women and was told the woman's body puts everything into fertility. When there is nothing else, the survival of the species instinct kicks in. If a western woman ate so little, she probably would not have periods. But it is because the poor women of Africa and India are now into that survival mode that they have a high fertility rate in spite of being so malnourished.

If something has changed, if women's fertility is an issue, then what is the UN doing about it? Just to put out a statement saying women have the right to control

---

37   Ellis *et al. Gender Equality and Growth Evidence and Action*, DFID, 2006.

their own fertility will not be enough. It needs to be backed up by funding and, of course, family planning education. And yet in 2008 President Bush blocked funding to NGOs that promoted family planning, somehow suggesting that they worked with the Chinese government, whom the US government accused of 'coercive abortion and involuntary sterilisations'. Marie Stopes International (MSI) put out a blistering statement rejecting the accusation and warning that the decision to discontinue the provision of US-funded contraceptive commodities to MSI would 'seriously disrupt' their family planning programmes in at least seven countries including Ghana, Kenya, Malawi, Sierra Leone, Tanzania, Uganda and Zimbabwe. MSI's chief executive, Dana Hovig, said women in these countries would be left with few options other than abortion, the majority of which would be unsafe and would be likely to result in their death or disability. He added: 'At a time when world governments have pledged to increase their commitment of improving the health of women, only the Bush Administration could find logic in the idea that they can somehow reduce abortion and promote choice for women in China by causing more abortion and cutting choice for women in Africa.'

Between 2002 and 2008, the Bush Administration withheld a total of US$235 million authorised by Congress to the UNFPA (United Nations Population Fund), which supports family planning and reproductive health care programmes in 154 countries.[38] That funding would have prevented 244,000 maternal deaths, helped 68 million women delay pregnancy and prevented 2.4 million women suffering from adverse health effects during pregnancy and childbirth, according to Anika Rahman, president of a New York-based group set up in 1998 to supplement funding lost to the UNFPA as a result of the Bush decision.

Happily, in his first days in office President Barack Obama rescinded the Bush rulings saying: 'they have undermined efforts to promote safe and effective voluntary family planning in developing countries. For these reasons, it is right for us to rescind this policy and restore critical efforts to protect and empower women and promote global economic development.'

A good first step, but Obama and all world leaders face vast financial problems, and the genuine concern is that the priority will become inward-looking as banks, corporations and countries retreat to their borders to try to salvage something from the wreckage. As UN Secretary General Ban Ki-moon said in October 2008: 'while the financial crisis affects all countries, the poor in developing countries will be the worst hit.'

On the positive side, perhaps the truth is finally out: if you cannot control your own fertility, you cannot control you own life. Now the important factor is how do

---

38   UK All Party Parliamentary Group on Population Development and Reproductive Health.

women get to control their own fertility? You can't say to a woman that she must have control of her own fertility and just expect it to happen. How do they get to the point where women can understand about their own bodies? They need to know what they should do and why it is critical they take certain steps. It is a journey of understanding, but it requires that initial financial impetus.

How is it that we can be living in the 21st century and still be tolerating violence against half the population on a scale which even in the darkest days of past history has never been seen: forced marriage, dowry deaths, female infanticide, the abortion of female foetuses, marital rape, forced pregnancy, sterilisation, trafficking, honour killings and prostitution? It is getting worse, not better. Globalisation may have opened the world up but it has also given a boost to some of these horrors, particularly trafficking and prostitution. Poverty is often at the root of much misery when parents are so poor that they sell their daughter for something to eat and in the hope that she will enjoy a better life – she seldom does.

There are glimmers of hope, and we have to seize on those when they appear. In October 2008, a West African court found Niger's government guilty of failing to protect a woman from slavery. Hadijatou Mani was sold when she was 12, raped aged 13 and forced to bear her 'master's' children, and made to work for ten years. Whenever she ran back home, she was always returned to her slave master. The government of Niger was ordered to pay her the equivalent of £12,430. What was striking for me was what she intended to do with the money. She said: 'I will be able to build a house, raise animals and farm land to support my family. I will also be able to send my children to school.'

But such moments are rare and only serve to highlight the extent of the problem. I would like to distinguish between a parent selling a child for what amounts to food and a consensual arranged marriage – what some in the West may regard, incorrectly as forced marriage. If a girl in Pakistan were to be married to her cousin, for example, she might not have any say in the matter. In that sense many marriages are forced. In a village, if the parents said to their daughter that she was going to marry a certain man, she would not be able to say no. She has not been brought up to do that and, what is more, it would probably not enter her head to refuse. She may not like it, but she would accept it because no one has told her she has a right to refuse. Such marriages are not right in rural communities even where there is ignorance, and certainly not right when families settle in the West. In the UK, the Home Office has received hundreds of calls on its hotline from girls frightened because they are being forced into marriage, and they have followed up some 500 cases.

We have come to accept that African conflicts will result in terrible violence. As I write this chapter, the Democratic Republic of Congo is once again experiencing war, and one commentator has said that we have become so used to Africa fighting that it rarely makes the headlines or even captures the full attention of the international community currently preoccupied with Iraq, Afghanistan or the economy. But while these events go on, children are being kidnapped and turned into little soldiers, women are being raped and killed, and men too are being hacked to pieces.

Don't think violence is confined to the battlefield. Domestic violence and sexual violence in homes – so-called intimate partner violence – is endemic in every country throughout the world. According to an international survey by UNICEF, between 20 per cent and 50 per cent of women in every country suffer from some form of domestic violence.[39] Every country passes laws supposedly to protect women, but if a woman has no value in a particular country, why should those laws be enforced? Such laws can also be something of a catch-all encompassing everything from pushing and shouting to breaking bones and rape – even within marriage. It is a scandalous statistic that domestic violence causes more death and disability among women aged 15 to 45 than cancer, malaria, traffic accidents and war, according to the Human Rights Watch Report 2000. Another grim statistic reveals that between 40 per cent and 70 per cent of murders of women are committed by their husband or boyfriend.[40]

I recall listening to a panel of western speakers addressing women's issues in Kenya, and one was saying how they had been trying to get women's health further up the agenda but couldn't persuade the health ministry to treat it as a priority. I said to them: 'How can you expect that to happen when women have no value?' They started writing this down as though they had discovered something for the first time. Perhaps they had, but I am shocked at the lack of awareness or understanding by these high-powered representatives who attend such meetings. They know all the statistics about how much money is being spent by the health ministry or how much aid is getting through, but they don't know why women's health is not on the agenda. Women don't matter to the men in power. That is why it is not yet on the agenda. But it is not just violence against women, it is also ignorance. The almost casual disregard for women has become a way of life. One survey conducted by DFID in Malawi found that 25 per cent of women thought the violence they endured from their husbands was legal.

In 2007 the World Health Organization reported that somewhere in the world one woman dies every minute of the day from causes related to pregnancy and childbirth, and this despite the fact that modern medicine can and should eradicate maternal mortality. In sub-Saharan Africa risks are even higher, and the maternal death rate is 1 in 16 compared with 1 in 2,800 in developed countries. Nigeria, with

39 UNICEF, *Domestic Violence Against Women and Girls*.
40 World Health Organization.

1,100 maternal deaths per 100,000 live births, is the worst example in Africa, and only exceeded by India. Nigeria is home to 2 per cent of the global population, but 10 per cent of all maternal deaths occur there. WHO also report that even if women survive the births, there are still 300 million living with pregnancy-related illnesses. And what does the future hold for the children? The reality for nine million every year is a life of hunger and misery until they die of malnutrition before their fifth birthday. Such a life is its own form of violence against defenceless people, and it stems directly from violence against women.

Let me return to my central theme – giving women the ability to earn just a few pennies to transform their lives and the lives of everyone around them. When Hadijatou Mani was released from a life in slavery and was paid the princely sum of a few thousand pounds for her torment, her first thought was to build a home and educate her children. Multiply that by a few million, and it immediately becomes apparent what could be achieved if women were told they had the right to take care of their own health and, as the UN has demanded, were given control of their own fertility. With some small financial independence and some dignity restored, the position of that woman does not become equal to a man's but she gains a value in her own eyes and in the eyes of her family and the village. When others see what she has achieved, soon the whole village is transformed. They start to take an interest in building up a future because they gain influence through the fact that they are not just downtrodden and valueless. I myself have witnessed many times the transformation that can be achieved and the wide-ranging consequences.

6

THE MILLENNIUM DEVELOPMENT GOALS

There is nothing any right-thinking person could say against the overall concept of the eight Millennium Goals. Their basic aim is encapsulated in the first goal: to reduce hunger and poverty around the globe. How can anyone possibly disagree with such a noble concept? We all support it. At the United Nations Millennium Summit in 2000, 189 countries signed up to the goals and many major businesses were quick to add their names to the cause. And then what?

As I write this, we are more than halfway to the target date of 2015 when the goals should be achieved, and clearly we are never going to make it. Let me make a prediction: when we get to 2015 we will quietly have to extend the target date, we will rephrase the goals and we will inevitably have another 'major' conference to discuss how urgent the problems are. Either that or we will quietly forget all about the MDGs. In the meantime thousands more will have suffered and millions more will have been born – the two facts are inseparable, but we are afraid to admit it. It is high time we faced the real facts of life. And despite all the speeches that have been made, the research carried out and the data published, one fundamental fact is that most people have never even heard of the Millennium Development Goals, and if they have, they would not be able to list them.

So what are the goals and their underlying targets?

Goal 1: Eradicate extreme poverty and hunger—the aim is to halve, between 1990 and 2015, the proportion of people whose income is less than $1 a day; to achieve full and productive employment and decent work for all, including women and young people, and halve, between 1990 and 2015, the proportion of people who suffer from hunger.

Goal 2: Achieve universal primary education—the target is to ensure that, by 2015, children everywhere, boys and girls alike, will be able to complete a full course of primary schooling.

Goal 3: Promote gender equality and empower women—the intention is to eliminate gender disparity in primary and secondary education, preferably by 2005, and in all levels of education no later than 2015.

Goal 4: Reduce child mortality—by reducing by two thirds, between 1990 and 2015, the under-five mortality rate.

Goal 5: Improve maternal health—the targets are to reduce by three quarters the maternal mortality ratio and to achieve universal access to reproductive health care.

Goal 6: Combat HIV/Aids, malaria and other diseases—to have halted by 2015, and begun to reverse, the spread of HIV/Aids; to achieve by 2010 universal access to treatment for HIV/Aids for all those who need it; and to have halted by 2015, and begun to reverse, the incidence of malaria and other major diseases.

Goal 7: Ensure environmental sustainability—the aim is to integrate the principles of sustainable development into country policies and programmes and reverse the loss of environmental resources; reduce biodiversity loss, achieving by 2010 a significant reduction in the rate of loss; halve by 2015 the proportion of the population without sustainable access to safe drinking water and basic sanitation; and by 2020 to have achieved a significant improvement in the lives of at least 100 million slum dwellers.

Goal 8: Develop a global partnership for development—the aim is to address the special needs of the least-developed countries, landlocked countries and small island developing states; develop further an open, rule-based, predictable, non-discriminatory trading and financial system; deal comprehensively with developing countries' debt; in cooperation with pharmaceutical companies, provide access to affordable essential drugs in developing countries; in cooperation with the private sector, make available the benefits of new technologies, especially information and communications.

This is an ambitious programme and, as I say, few would disagree with its intentions. Individual countries have undoubtedly made progress in achieving some of the targets. In 2002 the UN Development Programme Bureau reported substantial improvement in education in Guinea and Malawi and in overall nutrition in Indonesia and Tunisia. But in other countries child mortality rates have increased. Where one country achieves success in improving access to clean drinking water, another nation fails; where disease is reduced in one region, HIV/Aids rises alarmingly in another.

What worries me greatly is that even where there is progress the numbers are often not put up against the most frightening statistic of all: the huge rise in the population. If four million more children are in school, have we made any progress if another four million have been born? No one is prepared to acknowledge the reality; everyone talks about child mortality, but no one will point to the population growth in many of these developing countries. How can you help child mortality and maternal health unless you give the women the chance to have fewer children? You will never catch up with the number of children being born to undernourished women, many of whom are being driven from place to place because of wars in their regions. It is tragic to see these starving babies clinging to their mothers, but why are they being born in the first place in those appalling conditions? It would help the mother and her existing children, and certainly save the pain and suffering of that little mite, if it had never been born in the first place. In other words, the numbers we are reading about – even the better ones – are not reliable.

The MDGs do form a real programme for improvement, but in fact fewer goals could achieve just the same: improving the lives of women through employment of some kind would make many of the goals happen by default. There is another legitimate complaint made about the MDGs. Some countries are richer than others, and to set generalised targets may fail to recognise achievement when it has been made. According to the 2007 UN report on Africa and the Millennium Development Goals: 'At the midway point between their adoption in 2000 and the 2015 target date for achieving the Millennium Development Goals, sub-Saharan Africa is not on track to achieve any of the Goals.' One observer, William Easterly, a New York University economist and visiting fellow at the Brookings Institution's Global Economy and Development Program, said, this is unfair to poorer countries. The problem, Easterly argues, is that targets were originally established as a set of benchmarks to evaluate global trends; instead the measures are now being applied to individual countries. In short, it is tougher for poorer countries to hit the targets, and I would give the benefit of the doubt to all countries where at least some people are trying to make a difference. However, as I see it, the bar has been set too high and there is a cheaper and easier alternative. They have developed this agenda that is impossibly ambitious – I doubt whether 10 per cent has been achieved as I write this. No one has done any detailed analysis or inter-country comparisons. And still we are not focusing on the basis on which the goals could be brought about. If we continue to be stubborn about this, they will never be reached.

The common denominator of all these goals, and the key to making them work, is women. Yet one of the most distressing aspects of the speeches given by the British Prime Minister, Gordon Brown, and the UN Secretary General, Ban Ki-moon, at a meeting in New York in September 2008 aimed at accelerating global progress on the Millennium Development Goals, was that they barely mentioned the 'W' word. Are women not half the population, and aren't women the poorest of the poor? Women are the ones suffering the most in the world, but they scarcely merit a passing reference in the debate at these grand meetings.

In fact, it was left to Gordon Brown's wife, Sarah, to say what needed to be said, when she gave a speech as patron of the White Ribbon Alliance for Safe Motherhood. She opened her comments at an event discussing the Commitment to Progress for Mothers, Newborns and Children with the words: 'As far as I know, this is the first time such an event has taken place and the first time that the health of mothers and children has been seriously on the table for so many powerful people. That is a great achievement.' She hit the nail firmly on the head when she said: 'If you save mothers, you improve the chances of children.'

When he was UN Secretary General, Kofi Annan put it plainly: 'It is impossible to realize our goals while discriminating against half the human race.' Of the eight goals, poverty, education and health have been identified as the three requiring the most urgent action – all three can be improved if women are helped to take care of their own income, their own bodies and the future of their children.

Soon after they were adopted, everyone seemed to accept that the MDGs could not be met unless they were focused on women. So why has that notion now disappeared? It is perfectly clear, if you read each goal, that concentrating on women is the key, but seven or eight years later only Liberia and Denmark say their goals are women-centred. What has happened? Have people forgotten that the goals are supposed to put women at the heart of the debate, or have they decided that it is going to upset the countries they are working in? Are there political reasons why the emphasis has shifted away from women?

Let us just look at the list. The first goal addresses poverty and hunger. Do men put food in the starving children's mouths? No one speaks about the women farmers. If men were going to find and prepare the food, they would surely have done it by now. It was a terrible disappointment that the meeting of heads of state in New York had so little to say about how women should become the focus of all this effort. If you help women earn some money, they will ensure that the family is not hungry because the men are often not there, especially in Africa, to feed the family. It is much more likely if you work with women at this very basic level that they will succeed where men have not. Men have had all the life chances that are going in every corner of the world. If it is not working, as it surely is not, then whose fault can it be? And still people are not prepared to let the other half of the population have an opportunity to put matters right.

The second goal on primary education is all about women, and yet the importance of that role is not mentioned. It is the mother who wants to ensure that her children are educated in order to give them a better chance in life than she has had. One hopes that, unlike their husbands, the mothers will make no distinction between boy and girl; they may even make an extra effort for their daughters because they don't want them to suffer as they themselves have done. They know that their sons will always have a head start because it is, after all, a man's world.

The third goal, to promote gender equality and empower women, is a fundamentally flawed notion, and an indication of how little is understood about women in developing countries. If you set a goal to empower women, you immediately cut across the grain of so much of society where the male is dominant, and the only consequence of such action will be to create resistance. You cannot foist equality on people from the outside and say 'now you are equal', and somehow they will have magically achieved equality. It doesn't work like that. What is going to make women become equals? If the goals of the MDGs are focused on women then women will eventually achieve equality by themselves. You cannot just focus on gender equality. In fact that is the wrong way to work in societies where people are nervous about equality; indeed such an approach is only likely to antagonise the male population. A mother in a slum in Africa or India does not strive for empowerment or even know what that means; it is not the first thing on her mind when she wakes up in the morning. Her first thought is survival: food and water. Her priority is her children and her husband, and finally herself. Empowerment and equality will follow quite naturally when a woman has achieved these basics as a result of having the chance to earn a little money. Everything else will fall into place. You cannot race to the finishing line without taking that first step. Somehow we must create the conditions in which women can acquire some modest status or at least the ability to manage their own lives. They will take the equality themselves, when the time comes and when they are ready. To that end the commitments made by Robert Zoellick, President of the World Bank, at the same MDG forum in September 2008 to improve the integration of women into World Bank agriculture and development projects are nearer the mark. Political empowerment is for a later day: for now, it is meaningless.

The fourth goal, to reduce child mortality, is again putting the focus in the wrong place. If you give women control over their own fertility then clearly there will be less mortality because there will be fewer mouths to feed, fewer children being born infected with disease. Is it better to have a dead baby than not to have that baby in the first place? Instead of focusing on why children are dying – that is obvious: they are sick and hungry – ask why are there so many children. Hungry mothers with hungry children do not want or need more children.

The fifth goal, to improve maternal health and reduce maternal mortality, relates to the same point: fewer children, particularly born to young women who are no more than girls, must surely be the answer. But notice how maternal health is the fifth goal and child health the fourth goal. Is a child's health more important than the mother's? No, improve the mother's health first and then the child's health will improve as a result. The target to reduce the maternal mortality ratio by three quarters is said to be the goal least likely to be achieved by 2015. If the population of Africa is going to more than double in the next 40 years, how can we ever meet such targets? It is beyond any reasonable or logical thinking. It is not rational to believe that you are going to improve people's lives if the population is going to expand so rapidly. To improve maternal health women have got to stop having so many children, particularly those women who are already sick or hungry and probably both. I believe that keeping a woman pregnant is a way of keeping her under a man's control. It always has been a means of control and also a reflection on man's virility. He doesn't see the chaos of having so many children because he doesn't make himself responsible for looking after the children or sorting out the chaos in the home. He leaves it to his wife to manage. If there are a few rupees to go round and to be divided into six or seven, he is not going to be bothered that his wife now has to find a way of dividing the same amount of money among eight. Why do they have more children? Because that is what he has been told is his job. If you have a big family, everyone else will think you are a real man. If it were just the sex then would he not be willing to use a condom?

The sixth goal, to combat Aids and other diseases, is of course directly linked to MDG 5 as well. The Bush idea to promote abstinence is not the answer, and I think the least said about that proposition the better. Unless we make population an issue – make the use of condoms part of the drive to reduce the population increase and to cut the incidence of HIV – then I fear for humankind itself, never mind trying to achieve some particular goal. The reality is that population growth is feeding all these diseases – we have to be prepared to confront that inescapable and growing fact of life. Part of the goal is to improve access to treatment, which must be right, but I would focus more on prevention than cure. Again this is where the business community can make an impact.

The seventh goal is striving for environmental stability, and the targets concern sustainable development in policies and programmes to reverse the loss of national resources, improve access to safe drinking water and improve the lot of millions living in slum dwellings. It is as plain as a pikestaff that the one certain way to improve all three is to halt the population explosion. Do the environmentalists believe that these issues have nothing to do with the population increase? The earth may be a large place but we gravitate to centres of prosperity. We are warned that oil is running out, that the air is choked with fumes from cars and industry. The logic is compelling to me and should be to everyone else. What more proof do we need?

Finally, we have the global partnership for development. The presumption implied is that we all believe in development. Who is going to say that they don't? But what is development? It seems to have nothing to do with women; in fact, it seems to be about everything else other than women. The policy makers want to tackle the debt problems of developing countries, create affordable access to essential drugs and make new technologies available to developing countries. My argument is, why make everything so complicated? The solution to so many of the problems being targeted can be narrowed down to a common theme. Setting the goals and trying to galvanise the international community into some form of coordinated action are good ideas in principle, because at least they raise awareness among people. But I doubt whether they raise awareness of the fact that women are at the heart of the issue.

Just in case some might think my pessimism about achieving the MDGs is just the ramblings of a solitary figure, the British Parliament published a report on the impact of the goals on population growth back in January 2007. The UK All Party Parliamentary Group on Population, Development and Reproductive Health took high level evidence from academia, the United Nations, charities, the World Health Organization, the World Bank and the International Monetary Fund, among many others. They had all the expertise before them and concluded that the goals 'will be difficult or impossible to achieve with current levels of population increase in the least developed countries'. And perhaps most conclusive of all, their report stated: 'The MDGs failed to take into account the population growth factor. This has significant negative impacts on socio-economic development, human health, regional stability and the environment.' And one of its Key Findings made this blunt statement: 'No country, with the exception of a few oil-rich states, has risen from poverty whilst still having high fertility rates – which also impact directly on levels of maternal and child mortality.' It is also worth recording that among the Parliamentary Group's main recommendations was that the availability of contraceptive supplies be a priority, and barriers to the use of family planning should be eliminated – in stark contrast to the Bush Administration's approach.

The Group reached all the right conclusions, pointing out that lower birth rates will enable greater savings, investment and productivity per capita – even going so far as to say this is precisely what East Asia achieved – but then pulled their punch. To me, the next blindingly obvious step would be to say that you cannot talk about population growth without focusing on women.

A few months later, on 31 July 2007, some 60 companies signed up to what was called the Business Call to Action Declaration, committing themselves to stop talking about the need for change and to start taking action. They all agreed at the time that the world was not on track to achieve the MDGs by 2015. They stated:

> We need to mobilise all our efforts. The eighth Millennium pledge was that we would 'develop a global partnership for development'. The time has come for us all to live up to that promise. We believe we now need an international effort that harnesses the power of everyone: the private sector, individuals, consumers, faith groups, cities, civil society organisations, as well as governments, north and south, to work together to achieve the Millennium Development Goals.

Well, of course, as everyone accepts, the goals will not be achieved; but at least big business appeared to be galvanised to help. My aim in this short book is to ensure that efforts are directed where they can have the maximum effect.

I have no doubt that the only way we are going to make real progress is by harnessing the potential of big business. Just as Robert Zoellick of the World Bank said he wanted to increase the focus on the role of women in all the bank's projects, so must the other names who signed the Declaration. A reminder to them and everyone else who they are:

(1)   Cynthia Carroll, Chief Executive, Anglo American plc

(2)   Riley Bechtel, Chairman and Chief Executive Officer, The Bechtel Corporation

(3)   Gunter Thielen, Chairman and Chief Executive Officer, Bertelsmann AG

(4)   John T. Chambers, Chairman and Chief Executive Officer, Cisco Systems

(5)   Chuck Prince, Chairman and Chief Executive Officer, Citigroup

(6)   Nicky Oppenheimer, Chairman, De Beers Group

(7)   Paul Walsh, Chief Executive Officer, Diageo

(8)   Frederick W. Smith, Chairman, President and Chief Executive Officer, FedEx

(9)   Jeff Immelt, Chief Executive Officer, GE

(10)   Lloyd Blankfein, Chairman and Chief Executive Officer, The Goldman Sachs Group Inc.

(11)   Dr Eric Schmidt, Chief Executive Officer and Chairman of the Executive Committee, Google Inc.

(12)   Bernard Arnault, Chairman, LVMH

(13)   Ian E. L. Davis, Worldwide Managing Director, McKinsey & Company, Inc.

(14)   Bill Gates, Chairman, Microsoft

(15)   Indra Nooyi, President and Chief Executive Officer, PepsiCo Inc.

(16)   Sir Niall Fitzgerald, Chairman, Reuters Group plc

(17)   Graham Mackay, Chief Executive, SAB Miller

(18)   Ratan Tata, Chairman, The Tata Group

(19)   Patrick Cescau, Group Chief Executive, Unilever PLC/Unilever N.V.

(20)   Arun Sarin, Chief Executive Officer, Vodafone

(21)   H. Lee Scott Jr, President and Chief Executive Officer, Wal-Mart Stores, Inc.

(22)   Keith Clarke, CEO, Atkins

(23)   Sam Laidlaw, Chief Executive, Centrica plc

(24)   Mark Foster, Group CEO, Accenture

(25)   Richard Lambort, CBI

(26)   Neville Isdell, Chairman and Chief Executive Officer, The Coca-Cola Company

(27)   Deborah Leary, CEO, Forensic Pathways

(28)   Pramath Raj Sinha, 9.9 Mediaworx Pvt Ltd

(29)   Colin Melvin, Chief Executive, Hermes Equity Ownership Service (EOS)

(30)   Rod McDonald, Chairman, Buro Happold

(31)   Peter Marks, CEO, The Co-Operative Group

(32)   Bjorn Stigson, President, World Business Council for Sustainable Development

(33)   Yogesh Chander Deveshwar, Chairman of the Board, ITC (India)

(34)   Carl Henric Svanberg, Telefonaktiebolaget LM Ericsson

(35)   Stephen Rubin, Chairman, Pentland Group plc

(36)   Peter Sands, Group Chief Executive, Standard Chartered

(37)   Marius Kloppers, CEO, BHP Billiton

(38)   Peter Chernin, Chief Operating Officer and President, News Corporation

(39)   Matthew Key, Telefonica

(40)   Justin King, CEO, Sainsbury's

(41)   John Varley, CEO, Barclays

(42)   John Young, Pfizer

(43)   Hiromasa Yonekura, President, Sumitomo Chemical Co. Ltd

(44)   Ozwald Boateng, Bespoke Couture Ltd

(45)   Paul Batchelor, Chairman, Crown Agents

(46)   Peter Gammie, Group Chief Executive, Halcrow

(47)   Stefan Oschmann, President, Human Health, Europe, Middle East, Africa, Canada, Merck & Co.

(48)   Shoei Utsuda, President and CEO, Mitsui & Co. Ltd

(49)   Bradford A Mills, Chief Executive, Lonmin plc

(50)   Paul Skinner, Chairman, Rio Tinto plc

(51)   David Williams, CEO, Impact International

(52)   Sandra Macleod, Chief Executive, Echo Research Ltd

(53)   Frederico Fleury Curado, CEO, EMBRAER

(54)   Jayant Pendharkar, Vice President, TATA

(55)   Gautam Singhania, Chairman and MD, Raymond Limited

(56)   Kevin Horak, MD, Clearwater Special Projects Ltd

(57)   Larry Magor, CEO, Biwater

(58)   Geoffrey French, Chairman, Scott Wilson Group plc

(59)   Lord Michael Hastings CBE, Global Head of Citizenship and Diversity, KPMG International

(60)   James Smith, Chairman, Shell

If only just a few of those impressive names can apply the right pressure on their local operations in developing countries then great things could be achieved. But a note of caution: so much money and effort has been pledged, particularly by governments, but we don't really know where it is all going. Who is benefiting? What are the results? With such distinguished names as we now have on board, one can only hope that the auditing of the billions of dollars in aid will be rigorous. I fear a large percentage will never reach its intended target, but if the emphasis is right – that is, on women – then, as I have argued, it will not be long before we witness the start of a significant change.

Now I accept that you cannot halt a UN behemoth in full flow, but I would like to suggest some specific amendments to give the MDGs a more relevant and sharper focus. It is perfectly possible for the MDGs to be varied – Cambodia has its own CDGs (Cambodia Development Goals) which it believes are less ambitious and more realistic.

The MDGs should be adapted, and countries encouraged to prioritise the goals according to their national needs. There is no reason why they should be immutable, since every country is different. If we can stop violence against women in, for example, sub-Saharan Africa, we will be achieving something very important. If we can help women to protect themselves from HIV in South Africa, we will be reaching a hugely significant goal in all senses: medically, economically and socially. If we can stop health workers being raped and infected in Swaziland – which recently overtook Botswana as the country with the highest known prevalence of HIV/Aids in the world – then that is a major milestone. The point is that the goals have been formulated by people who sit in offices, but do they know what is happening on the ground in each country? It is essential that countries modify the goals to suit their own situation; more than that, they need to prioritise them and use the MDGs as a guide. With that sort of focus, each country would start making some real progress. But the world leaders are not articulating the most appalling aspect. They meet together, but they never address the central point: the MDGs are unrealistic, and some, such as women's empowerment and equality, are not only far-fetched but also counter-productive. It is perfectly plain that, unless you first help the mothers, none of the goals will be reached – least of all the ambition for empowerment and equality.

My suggested additions and amendments to the Millennium Development Goals are:

(1) **Every aid initiative must include and be tested for effectual provisions for women**—every aid initiative must include provisions specifically for women. Every aid initiative must then be monitored to ensure the initiative is being effective in its scope, method and success. If someone wants to build a dam or a new school, the developer must be asked how this impacts on women and specifically what roles will be set aside for women under the new scheme. Women do not need to be running the project, but they could be running a canteen for workers. The UK's Department for International Development states that they have no initiative which does not have gender considerations built in, but I would push for the consideration to be at the very top of the agenda, not an adjunct, with a provsion for auditing and monitoring the implementation of policies.

(2) **The gender balance to be either equal or tipped in favour of women for all initiatives**—I propose initiatives being openly in favour of women. This is a more powerful statement that will bring greater action and a greater return.

(3) **Fifty per cent of all aid should go to women-centric projects**—this is an ambitious target but no more ambitious than the existing MDGs. We have established that there is a dire need for aid because all the developing nations are blighted by hunger, poverty and disease. Bearing the brunt of all this are women, but if we devise a way of ensuring that women are directly compensated then the transformation will be instantaneous, and perhaps the MDGs in many countries will become a possibility even if we miss the exact target date. A recent census in India clearly proved how infant mortality was inversely related to a mother's educational level. While it is generally accepted that there is a direct correlation between illiteracy, high levels of fertility and mortality, I maintain that there is an even greater correlation between income generation and these conditions. Income, however small, leads to an immediate change. According to the US-based The Hunger Project:

> The persistence of hunger and abject poverty in India and other parts of the world is due in large measure to the subjugation, marginalization and disempowerment of women. Women suffer from hunger and poverty in greater numbers and to a greater degree than men. At the same time, it is women who bear the primary responsibility for actions needed to end hunger: education, nutrition, health and family income.

(4) **Every company seeking to work in a country must demonstrate creating and developing jobs for women**—this does not mean they should be given board positions or be senior executives, but just insisting on asking this question as a first step: where do women fit in your company's plans? Such a requirement would not affect the commercial decision to build a factory but it would begin to redress the balance. It should surely be possible to find work for at least ten women a year. Remember this is not just providing work for ten women – there is the multiplier factor: ten women earning money probably means 30 children being fed, that is hundreds of dollars a year not being spent on medicine for malnourished infants, that is many more children attending schools and they in turn being able to contribute to their communities and society, increasing the wealth of their villages. All this can be achieved just by letting a handful of women earn a tiny fraction of the cost of a project.

(5) **Crime against women – a financial penalty**—violence against women is a worldwide phenomenon but the penalties are at best ineffective at stopping the epidemic. I would like to see women receiving some financial compensation when the courts prove that a woman has been abused or attacked. If the perpetrator of the attack knows that his pay packet will be directly affected then he might think twice. This is not as unrealistic as it may sound. As we have seen, if it is possible for a single woman who has been held as a slave, raped and abused for years to take the Niger government to court and win then anything is possible. Violence against women can only be stopped by punitive financial penalties. We should remind ourselves that violence against women is a universal issue. Many men in the western, 'developed' world are treating women appallingly but at least the women have some choices. In poorer countries they have no choices, and to me that is a key factor. If a women is treated badly in the UK she doesn't have to put up with it. She can ask for help or at least tell somebody. She may not have the courage to do it but she does have the choice.

(6) **Every woman should have access to testing for Aids**—businesses must take their responsibilities seriously about the health not only of their employees but also of the wider community in which they are working. They should go further than just putting up notices in their factories warning about the dangers of Aids, and any company over a certain size should, based on the number of employees, provide clinics which would be open not only to their workers but to their spouses and the local community upon whom the businesses depend to a greater or lesser extent. This would be the best use of their corporate social responsibility.

Of all these suggestions, the most vital and the least expensive is for chief executives to ask themselves: what are we doing for women in our workplace? This first question will generate shockwaves of change. It has nothing to do with empowerment or seeking to upset the status quo which places men at the top; it has nothing to do with equality, but it is about changing the mindset. 'Empowerment' and 'equality' are two words which should be anathema to anyone working in development because you cannot enforce equality and bring about empowerment from the top: it has to come from within. It is the individual who is empowered, the individual who attains equality.

What's in it for men? They will be able to enjoy better health for themselves and their families as the joint income grows. Their children will be better looked after, fed and educated. There is no reason for men to lose anything. As a result of their modest jobs women will ultimately gain more equality when they are ready, but that is the finish line, not the starting line. Women need the basics first, and when they have the basics and see their own worth they will start to feel empowered. You can't enforce empowerment or equality on any community; if you try to, you will surely fail. These ideas are not about trying to make men subservient. They will remain the masters; we, the women, just want a piece of the cake, because if we are happier and healthier it will ultimately contribute to men's well-being.

The only people who can bring about this change are businesses and development providers – the very names who have signed up to the Business Call to Action Declaration. There is no other way this process will even begin. There is no point talking to women's organisations, the intellectual types who can talk until the cows come home. Most of the clever women are not action-oriented. They tell you what is wrong, they can analyse to the point where you can't understand what they are saying, but where is the practical application? Focusing on women is not the same as talking to women's organisations, which everyone promised to do. If women's organisations could have done something by now they would have done so. Why bother with them? I know it sounds so topsy-turvy, but if women could have brought about change by now we wouldn't be having this debate. It is essential that you go to the male-dominated organisations because that is where the power lies.

No one has seen women as the answer to poverty although there is plenty of evidence if we only care to look. In fact only poor women are the answer to poverty. People have focused on women who are better off and better educated, and relied on women to change women's situations. You must not ask women's organisations, or educated or intellectual women, to change the lives of the poorest. They don't connect with them. They can be as apart from them as a European is from an Indian. So what has to be done is to get men to connect with women, because it is the men who hold the power and the authority. You have got to go to where the power is, not where the talk is. If we wait for women's organisations to bring about change then we will wait forever.

In May 2009 the UK All Party Parliamentary Group published an Update Summary on its earlier findings on population and the Millennium Development Goals and concluded:

New data show that the key message from the [earlier] report – that the MDGs will be difficult or impossible to achieve with current levels of population increase in the least developed countries – remains true, and that increased investment in voluntary family planning programmes can also make a significant contribution to emerging development priorities, including climate change, fragile or failing states, as well as existing priorities such as poverty elimination.[41]

Is anything happening, I wonder?

This is all about creating change through action; it is about getting people to think not in intellectual terms but in practical terms. What can be done in the context of real life where there is pitiless poverty, ill health and work without reward?

---

41 Report Update Summary of Hearings by the UK All Party Parliamentary Group on Population, Development and Reproductive Health , Westminster, London, May 2009.

7

CHILD LABOUR
– THE GREAT
TABOO

There is less value placed on life, in general, in India and Africa and, of course, much less value on a woman's life. Women suffer greatly and daily, and their pain is somehow accepted by the world as a fact of life and probably beyond anyone's control. But we would do well to remember when we look at the faces of young children staring pitifully up at the TV cameras, as in times of famine, that for every child there is a long and harrowing tale of suffering with a woman at its heart.

Although the purpose of this book is to focus on women, I want to dwell for a moment on the children who are equally downtrodden but are also a vital source of revenue to impoverished families. We cannot think that we can impose the standards and practices of the developed world on developing countries. It won't work, and the sooner we realise that the sooner life will change for the better for many thousands of children and their families. Just as I want to change the mindset of people in their attitude and treatment of women, it should also be possible to change our attitude towards child labour.

According to Indian government statistics, there are 20 million child labourers in the country. I would not be surprised if the figure were more than double that, as other agencies claim. There is a law in India which makes it illegal to employ someone under 14 years of age unless they are working within a family environment, but like so many other laws in India it is flouted. According to the International Labour Organization, there are 250 million children aged between 5 and 14 who are working for a living in developing countries – nearly half of them full time.

The simple truth is that in communities where people are poor, children have to work. It is impossible for families to manage without the help of their children. So if a child is not going to school then he or she is working. It is a matter of survival. What we should be focusing on is children's working conditions. Rather than having them slaving in sweatshops, legitimate and respectable companies could find ways of employing these children for a maximum of four to five hours, giving them a hot meal in the day and providing two hours of schooling. A fanciful dream, I know, for the worst sort of 'employers' in some backstreets, but a realistic proposition for legitimate businesses who would not need to pretend that they don't have children working for them. The children will still earn money for their families, they will be well nourished and they will be learning at the same time. What has to be stamped out is 12 hours in a backstreet sweatshop with scarcely a break.

Many would say these children should not be working at all, and they would be right in an ideal world, but we do not live in an ideal world. The children should be in school, but there are two problems here. First, how can their parents manage their lives without their children's labour? And second, most parents cannot even afford to send their children to school. It's the double whammy. It is hard to see how that circle can be squared, because the advantages of the child offering some help to the family are clear if their help leads to a better way of life in the future with improved prospects for the whole family. Child labour is not an optional extra – everyone, regardless of their age, is needed to help in whatever way they can. It is not a choice, it is a necessity.

Western standards cannot be applied unless we make the most impoverished as well off as the West, which is clearly not possible. We are rightly concerned about the conditions and hours children work and the fact that they don't get a good meal during the day. How can a child's health be maintained like that? It can't, and it is plain that the fitter the children, the better the nation. My contention is that we have to start somewhere. We must be pragmatic as well as practical. There is a difference between child labour and child slavery. In India young children are 'indentured' to other people. In fact they are sold into slavery – 'bonded labour' – because it is virtually impossible for the child or family to 'buy' their way out of the 'employment', and families are dependent on the meagre wages to survive. In the Middle East there is so much slavery, usually among immigrants who come to the cities in search of fortune – they are the people on whose backs the glittering apartment blocks, hotels and shopping malls are being built.

If at a stroke child labour were abolished the result would be even more deprivation and hunger. Let the children in Pakistan make the footballs and Indians make clothes all for sale to the western market, but at least be sure that their conditions are good, that they are fed, receive some education and learn a skill. This would give them a future and an opportunity to make the break from a life of poverty.

Once again I turn to the business community to use their influence. They have a corporate social responsibility which takes them beyond the confines of their offices and factories where their responsibility is only to their immediate workforce. What I am advocating, if we really want to do something about what amounts to child abuse, is for companies to go out into the cities where they operate and show some real social responsibility. This is all tied up with helping women to run small businesses where they could also employ youngsters under their supervision and care.

We have to start at the beginning, at the root cause. In Asia they have children with the expectation that, as soon as their sons and daughters are able, they will work and contribute to the family. It is what they perceive as the duty of the child. Not only is it a duty but it is also a necessity, both in the cities and in the rural and farming communities. The situation is far worse in the cities, where the sweatshops proliferate and offer virtually nothing in return. The sight of boys selling magazines and newspapers on the roadside, making sales of maybe Rs. 300 a day, are familiar. They, of course, are controlled by one man who would provide them with the magazines at the start of the day and take most of the profit at the end. Some have tried to tell me that it is like the ivory poachers in Africa. If people go on buying ivory, the trade will continue and elephants will continue to die, somehow suggesting that it is better for these children to earn nothing at all rather than be working in the streets. But it is a false comparison. Child labour is a tradition, but a tradition born out of necessity, and it will continue because the necessity continues. The only way to bring it to an end is if you change the economic situation in the family.

In the cities women are earning and may often be the only one in the family in any kind of paid work. But the men take the money and squander it while the children toil away in the sweatshops, maybe not even earning anything but paying off some debt. In the cities it is particularly important that businesses find ways of employing children in a much safer and productive environment where they can be given food and some schooling. That is the only way to change their lives.

Just one survey, by the International Labour Organization, offers an array of depressing statistics. More than four out of five working children receive no pay at all because the majority – about 70 per cent – work for their families, usually in agricultural activity. As well as in farming, children can be found working in mines and weaving carpets as well as in domestic service and, of course, prostitution. Many children work seven days a week without holiday and for long hours, leaving them no free time to rest. Typically girls work longer hours than boys and for less pay. While it is easy to point the finger at Africa and Asia, it is worth remembering that there are many child workers in the industrialised countries of Eastern and Central Europe,[42] and not so long ago we had child workers in what we now regard as the advanced West. We should remember that in not-so-distant times children worked in British mines and in factories. Women, too, toiled in harsh conditions doing menial work, but even so were not seen as part of the natural workforce.

Let us not look at the developing world through the eyes of an idealist. Children will work because they have to work; what we have to do is to improve conditions so that gradually their lives improve. It is up to companies to get over their squeamishness about employing children. It is seen as a great taboo, but what is the alternative? They will sit in a dirty sweatshop working for hours on end with no hope of escaping their torment. Far better to accept that if they have to work they do it in a decent environment: five hours of work with some food and two hours of schooling. Then they can still help their family in the evening if there is a need.

I can just imagine the bad press if an organisation like ICI, for example, began employing 30 children. But someone has to break the mould and show how the children could benefit from such a working environment rather than slaving in brutal conditions. All it will take to answer all the criticism is for one leader to make a stand and demonstrate what can be done. What would we prefer – boys sold into bonded labour and girls into prostitution? How can that be something anyone would want for a child? Far from getting a bad press, a company should be applauded for announcing that it is taking the initiative to take on a group of children and give them a chance in life. Yes, of course, the business can also make a profit, because everything I am suggesting has to be sustainable: charity can only go so far.

This is not a case of perpetuating child labour; it is a rather accepting the facts of life, appalling though they are, as a reality. It is creating a new generation of workers who are well nourished and educated. In fact you will be creating a new workforce

---

42 ILO Bureau of Statistics, Geneva.

which is confident, healthy and literate. If children are literate, they can build a better life for themselves. I am not talking about college and university education; if a child can read and write, that's education and it's enough. Numeracy and literacy means that the children cannot be cheated or treated as dumb animals. Again we tend to think in terms of western education – secondary school and further education. But for me, literacy is the only basic requirement. That ability alone will be a major advance. I am also in favour of adult literacy in the community. If there is a woman who can be taught to read, she will teach others in her village to read, and that tiny, precious gift can be passed on. I have seen this very thing happen in a village in Madhya Pradesh, where a woman having being elected head of her village council decided that the one thing she wanted to achieve was to make everyone literate, so she started a campaign called *Jai Akshar*, which loosely translates as 'Honour to the Alphabet', and encouraged everyone who was literate to teach someone else to read. In the end every adult in the village was reading. Just as *Jai Hind* was the slogan rallying people to rise up against foreign rule, *Jai Akshar* is the campaign to liberate people from illiteracy and ignorance. The difficulty is that women's lives are so overburdened that it would be difficult to find time for education, so here again business can help. Businesses manage to train their employees to do the simple tasks they require: why not also find time for a little reading and writing? I used to teach English to women during their lunch hour at businesses in Maidenhead. It is possible to find the time. The upside for the employer is a smarter, brighter workforce and, in time, a wealthier community. A wealthier community spends more, and so you have the virtuous circle.

In these straitened times businesses may say educating the workforce is not their responsibility. Perhaps not, but I suggest that they should see it as an opportunity quite apart from discharging a debt to the society in which they are operating. And what about the wives of all the executives (who are probably mostly men)? There used to be a tradition for what we once called ex-pat wives living abroad to do some charitable work, but I fear that tradition is on the decline. I went to one summer party attended by many Indian executives' wives and one of them said she taught. I was delighted and asked where, and she said rather grandly, 'a Montessori school.' That's not what I mean by teaching, helping children who are already many rungs up the ladder. Another one had a lifestyle shop, as so many of the wealthy women do; it seems to have become fashionable to have a 'little shop' just to keep oneself occupied and amused. It probably makes no real difference to them whether it is profitable or not. They don't seem to want to do anything for anybody who is really in need. I find this trend very depressing. They could be out teaching the least fortunate children the basics in how to read and count, because those very basic skills will utterly transform lives. It would make children infinitely more employable – yes, even as children – and it could set them on a career path that they would never normally have enjoyed.

One western or developed world practice I would employ is that of careful scrutiny and monitoring, not only to ensure that the children were not suffering, albeit now in a gilded cage, but also more particularly to share news of success stories. I would mark it a success if companies could demonstrate that their initiative was helpful to the children as well as being profitable, or at the very least breaking even. I believe this should be one corporate achievement which chairmen would want to shout about – it hardly represents a confidential matter that they have been able to achieve a positive balance between their commercial duty to their shareholders and their corporate social responsibility to their workforce and the community in which they are operating.

Children will work anyway: they have to. By creating a caring environment for them to work it may well also create a life for them to live. Make the leap of faith away from the attitudes of developed countries where it is not necessary for a child to work. If you apply those attitudes to the developing countries, you will deprive so many youngsters of that chance of a better life. By applying those attitudes and practices, which are completely unsuitable in developing countries, you are positively damaging the prospects of those children.

I would take the words of Sarah Brown, wife of the British Prime Minister, Gordon Brown, when she said: 'If you save mothers, you improve the chances of children' and extend the sentence by adding '… and if you improve the chances of the children, you also save mothers.' What I mean by that, of course, is that with a modicum of education and a better life, it is just possible that the young boys, as they grow into adults, will treat the young women they meet with respect. It may not work in every case, but what is certain is that if we continue with more of the same we cannot expect to see any change. It is clear to me that more of the same can only lead to disaster, which in today's age will be global in scale.

8

GLOBALISATION – PART OF THE SOLUTION

If business is one half of the solution to righting so many of the social and environmental wrongs of this world, then globalisation is the other half and together they will run this century. While governments can affect the state of affairs within their own borders, I do not believe that by themselves they will have sufficient influence to bring about the scale of change required. Global businesses are already influencing what is happening, particularly in developing countries, and only they will have the resources and independence needed.

Of course, if governments help rather than hinder the process then change will happen sooner, but I don't think we can rely on governments; in the past they have been resistant to introducing the right initiatives, if not plain hostile. Why would they want to upset the cosy status quo which has allowed them to feather their nests for so long? By contrast, businesses are in a position to control what they do, and if they don't like the environment in one particular country they can always pack up and find another more enlightened host.

All too often aid and charity get lost in the entrails of government bureaucracy – sometimes through plain corruption, sometimes just because of the dead hand of government machinations – and those who really need the money, the poor and the destitute, rarely see it. So an institution is needed which is far more in control of its own operations. A company is driven by profit. It is constantly monitoring performance through good financial practice. If the management see the firm's assets disappearing without explanation they will want to know why, will rapidly introduce change and, if necessary, will sack the culprits pilfering the money. Government doesn't work like that.

Everyone accepts that we are interdependent, living in a shrinking world. Pollution in one country affects us all; financial incompetence, as we witnessed all too clearly in 2008, can have an almost instant global impact. There is no hiding place, but on the plus side such transparency can work in our favour. If governments introduce an initiative, say to help generate new wealth, improve farming or provide clean drinking water, then obviously they can share that success with a worldwide audience instantaneously. But you rarely hear about totally innovative government-led projects which have been successful in this area. The only successful projects are NGO-led initiatives. They may be cooperatives or some other small-scale ventures producing goods for sale locally, but that is a drop in the ocean, and it is not going to bring about the necessary change. That change can only come about if it is done on a large scale; charities and NGOs don't have the resources to do it alone. The advantage of charities and NGOs is that they are operating all over the world, and if people want to know what works they should just look at the charity networks. There are plenty of examples, but we need more development of business models like SEWA or Grameen, and on a larger scale. This can only come about through the business world. It is the only way we can bring about real change in the long term.

I don't doubt for one moment the sincerity of people giving generously to charity, sending money to help a child who has to carry water for miles. But why are we doing that? We should be helping the child's mother to support all her children, not sending money so one of her children can be lifted out of poverty. I get quite worked up about these images of children, but I suppose they tug at people's heart strings in the way a picture of an adult woman might not. Give a few pence, and we can educate this child. But what is the sense or the logic in such a generous act? Give the mother the 60p a day, because then she will feed all her children and be able to send them all to school. It is time they started using women to tug at people's heart strings. If you help a woman to earn money, she will send her first and second child to school. If you work at the base line, the mother, you are going to help all her children. The mother is the universal key to the well-being of the entire family. You can't help one child at a time. Adopt a child! Why not adopt a woman? The charities are all so focused on the children. It looks good; it appeals to our emotions, like adopting a panda or a tiger. But you have to see how you can bring about long-term change, not fix on one person who has fallen down and pick them up. That person will be all right, but all the others are still lying on the ground.

Just as businesses constantly monitor their books, if they really believe in this concept then they will closely scrutinise these new enterprises. I also believe that they will very quickly see the impact of their work because it will be reflected in the community around them and, most importantly, it will show up as profit in their books. Remember, the whole basis of this idea is that small businesses can be created that will enable both women and the companies backing them to make money; it is part and parcel of their corporate social responsibility, but it is not charity. It is absolutely essential – as I have said before, but it merits repeating – that businesses must benefit. It might not be part of their core activity but they should approach it in a businesslike fashion. Any project must be sustainable if it is to survive and deliver over the long term.

There is an almost in-built reluctance in Africa and the sub-continent to employ women or even see them as part of the normal paid workforce; in developed countries women are everywhere working in every conceivable environment – they are even part of the front-line troops, much to the surprise of many civilians. They have managed – not without difficulty – to push themselves into the workforce. And yet although women sustain everything in the developing world – agriculture, the health and welfare of their families, labouring in all sorts of environments – they are not regarded as part of the 'normal' workforce. That is probably one of the most fundamental points which has got to change if we are to make progress.

The sensitivities of society and religion may dictate that men and women cannot work side by side, but that was also how life began in the factories in the West. What is the problem? The problem is the problem itself, not something that is insoluble. It is not an obstacle, just a stepping stone along the way: simply create segregated work areas. If women can be asked to carry bricks on building sites as they do in developing countries, why should they be considered unsuitable for less physically demanding labour? Why are they not trained as bricklayers, if they can carry bricks – which is the toughest part of the job and gets the least money?

Training is clearly important. There is always this argument which says women can't do these jobs because they aren't trained, but men are not born trained. If companies operating in India or Africa managed to overcome the child labour taboo and started employing boys and girls, they will soon have a trained workforce. All people have to be trained, and women are people. If you stop using words like 'equality' and 'empowerment', then men will stop feeling threatened. Men also worry that they will lose the complete control they have over the lives of their families. Well, that would not be such a bad thing, because when they control the lives of their families they don't actually do the best that can be done.

Maybe the members of the United Nations should remember the Mission Statement of its own Division for the Advancement of Women:

> Grounded in the vision of equality of the United Nations Charter, the Division for the Advancement of Women (DAW) advocates the improvement of the status of women of the world, and the achievement of their equality with men – as equal actors, partners, and beneficiaries of sustainable development, human rights, peace and security. Together with Governments, other entities of the United Nations system, and civil society, including non-governmental organizations, DAW actively works to advance the global agenda on women's rights, gender equality and the empowerment of women, and ensure that women's voices are heard in international policy arenas.

Are these really empty words – an impossible dream? I think we must accept that the UN is powerless to bring about this sort of change, which is why I am turning to the business community who have signed up to the Millennium Development Goals. If we take India, for example, where the rise of business is phenomenal and companies are becoming influential global operators, we ought to be able to look to them to see what practices they could adopt to bring about change. I know of companies that are trying to help, but the effort lacks consistency and it is not being done on a scale that would bring about any real change in society or deliver real benefit to the poorest people; and as I always keep saying, the poorest of the poor are the women. We must hope that companies will adopt practices which will actually bring about real change. I welcome the growth and success of India's enterprises, but we must never forget that India has more malnourished people than any other country in the world. The United Nations can set its goals, which every member country supports, but in my opinion it is failing to use its undoubted influence, certainly as far as women are concerned. It is difficult to see that women permeate the UN's thinking in any way. It is all very well having a separate, even dedicated branch for women, but that is precisely what it is: an adjunct, just a sop. Women should be part of the central thinking of the UN on its many different levels.

Just as globalisation can have its benefits, 'one world' also has its drawbacks, and when one nation catches an economic cold, or even a fever, today we all catch it.

The recession which has gripped us all is not going to be helpful, because naturally companies will hesitate to look beyond their core business or take on new initiatives when they are focused 100 per cent on survival. Bankers in particular will retrench, cut overheads, possibly even retreat to their own countries. But sometimes when you are in a dip that is just the time to try something new – it may actually help you out of a dip. In fact a slump may be precisely the right time to try new initiatives. It's no good saying that you will wait until the economic climate has improved. We have supposedly just been through a boom time, and nothing was done then, because when things are going well people are frightened of making a change. There is never a perfect time for trying something new, so why not do it now? I am not suggesting that this is the time for extravagance or large-scale investments: quite the reverse. The beauty of my proposal is that for a small investment a large return is possible. I am proposing a first step: if it is successful, it could grow into a large enterprise and everyone will benefit; if it should fail, little will have been lost in money, time or effort.

The advantage for a company, beyond just profit, is the good publicity resulting from helping many of those trapped in poverty. If an idea works, the concept can be shared with others all over the world. But it requires serious commitment, without which nothing can ever work. I scan the list of the great and the good who have signed up to the Millennium Development Goals and ask myself what has been the result. What tangible benefit has there been for just one individual family in Africa or India? Signatures on paper remain just that, paper commitments. If indeed they have done more, we should all be shouting about it and celebrating their achievements because the ideas can be replicated. If all the companies on that list just make one effort and launch just one venture, great changes can be brought about. The power of the businesses to make a difference is much greater than even they realise. They rightly focus on their businesses, but if they spend just a fraction of their time on seeing how they can employ women, the impact could be huge. To date, strangely, it is the banks who have set the pace for change, but now that they have been directly and strikingly affected by the economic crash they probably can't do more. The difference, though, is that the banks have been helping women earn money through money, but this cannot be the only way. The women ought to be able to earn money by labour and by producing something tangible for sale.

While we are looking at globalisation, we can't ignore the more predatory type of globalisation which countries like China are operating. China, of course, is an extreme example, because its only objective is to gather influence and acquire precious resources. It still has a command economy, not even pretending to embrace democracy, so its objectives must always be suspect when it offers to provide aid to its new African 'friends'. I see globalisation purely in terms of the benefit it brings to big business, allowing it to make money, yes, but where it can also exercise a global as well as localised social conscience and responsibility. The reason we need to look to big business is precisely because there is no other institution which could bring about change without putting itself at risk in any way and without drawing accusations of political opportunism.

My hope is that by harnessing the twin powers of the spirit of globalisation and the energy and enterprise of business we will be able to turn words into action. We don't need any more speeches or reports and expensive conferences; instead, we need to examine which projects are making a difference. If there are such projects, why isn't good practice being exchanged? Why are we still talking about what is to be done? Has nothing been done in the past seven or eight years? Has nothing been achieved? If it has, we need to know more about it so it can be repeated: how was it achieved, at what cost, what were the benefits, what impact did it have on reducing poverty, Aids, hunger, disease, how many more children received education? With these real facts, any business can pick up the baton and multiply the benefits. It should then be perfectly straightforward to establish a database of women-centric projects which are successful, so that they can be rigorously tested to see how they are benefiting both the company and the community, and so we can move closer to achieving the MDGs.

In order to be successful in a country, enterprises must be sensitive to the local customs – which in my view makes them ideal ambassadors to promote this agenda. It chimes with the findings of the United Nations Population Fund (UNFPA) report on the state of world population released in November 2008. Entitled *Reaching Common Ground: Culture, Gender and Human Rights*, the report stated: 'Development strategies that are sensitive to cultural values can reduce harmful practices against women and promote human rights including gender equality and women's empowerment.'

As I have said before, women's empowerment will follow all in good time, but I was heartened by the statement of the UNFPA's Executive Director, Thoraya Ahmed Obaid, which said: 'To be healthy throughout the life cycle – before pregnancy, during pregnancy and after pregnancy – is a human right.'

While we may be living in a 'globalised' society, we nevertheless have our differences and these must be respected and preserved. As the UNFPA says, by adopting a sensitive approach and working with cultures, effective strategies and practices can be developed while promoting human rights at the same time.

It's easy to criticise, and I know that there are many individuals and organisations working hard to help people in many different countries. But if I were put in charge of bringing about the changes I am advocating I would focus on specific areas within each country, and send a woman into the villages to talk to the women there. A man might need to go in too, as a courtesy to the male head of a community, but it takes a woman to understand another woman's needs. I would want to see what the women's lives were like: how did they live, and had they any money? I would see whether the children were getting any education – if there was even a school. I would want to understand what was happening on the ground before suggesting any goals, targets or plans. I would look at what businesses were operating already in the district and what opportunities for women there might be from those businesses. If there were none, I would consider what specific product might be needed in the community and try to persuade a suitable business to set up a joint venture or cooperative so that the villagers could sell the goods and the business could also enjoy some of the profit.

This is how, in a very modest way, I would start. It is not something you can wave a wand at and say everyone should do it like that. That is where mistakes are made, because every area will have different needs. Every nation will have different types of people available for work. But businesses which are there already could be making this sort of inquiry themselves. They could see which were the nearest villages and poorest communities around them and establish a small business venture that local women could run. Or they could see whether the women or young people could be employed in some part of their core business. They might consider adopting a village; the Chamber of Commerce in Calcutta at one time was doing just that, creating excellent work opportunities although they weren't focusing on women.

These may seem obvious suggestions, and you wonder whether people are not already going to the villages. Some may be, but they don't go and ask the women. Never mind the developing countries – every consultation with ethnic minorities in the UK is with males. There are no women at these meetings, because women are not so-called community leaders. Why should communities work only through community leaders? It is one of the most damaging aspects of ethnic minority consultations. Does the rest of the British population have a community leader? Who is he – Gordon Brown? At some point one has got to stop having community leaders and start just having communities where everyone has a voice. If the white British don't have community leaders, why should ethnic minorities in Britain, and why do we have to deal only with (male) community leaders in the villages of India?

Why is the wise one of the village always considered to be a man? The eldest and the wisest is synonymous with the one who is the most old-fashioned, the least forward-looking. He wants to maintain the status quo and is therefore precisely the wrong person to talk to. If you are stupid, you are stupid. If you are also old, you are just old and stupid. We do now at last have village governments in India, and some of them have women representatives, albeit a small number – and I do wonder if at times they are merely 'fronting' for men. But the empowerment comes from self-confidence, and self-confidence comes from the ability to earn money. It is not the same everywhere, sadly; in the UK some people have come to realise that they are better off not working. It has become the survival of the unfittest, much to the fury of the working people of Britain. In India they have large families, and that means more hands to help with the work; in the UK some women may have eight or nine children by different fathers with the sole intention of never doing a day's work in their lives. The world sometimes just looks upside down.

But our focus is on the people who are desperate to lift themselves out of poverty and who are prepared to work; it is an ethos that remains with them all their lives, even when they travel to the West and achieve their life's ambition. It struck me that somehow we had to bring about change, and if you concentrate on situations in poor countries there is nothing else left that hasn't been tried. It is almost as though this is the last ditch. And then the penny dropped – help the mothers and the girls, and the rest follows automatically. Just look back at the underlying themes of the MDGs which along the way seem to have been forgotten, and it becomes crystal clear. Everyone insists they are women-centric, but that is as far as they go. It seems to me that it is time to put the alleged underlying core of the MDGs into practice. Don't just say women are central: show that they are central by diverting just a tiny fraction of the effort, the aid, and above all the belief into women. After all, what is the alternative?

9

THE OPPOSITION

I am nothing if not a realist, always ready to face facts and the blunt truth as they cross my path, so let's consider for a moment the potential opposition to this idea as I can already hear the pencils being sharpened and the PCs whirring into action. First, let me say that I welcome every comment, every argument and every rejection just as much as I will accept any plaudits or approval. At the end of this book I will give some contact details where every reader can have their say for or against. I do not want to hide from the comments, precisely because I want to start the dialogue, even argument, which for too long has been avoided. If we still don't think there is a problem, we could just remind ourselves by reading the pages at the start of this book under the heading The World in Which We Live. If we accept nothing else, at least we should ask what we would do to correct some of these appalling statistics. I am certainly not proud, and will happily support any and every alternative to the way we are running our lives at the moment. Even if readers disagree with everything else, surely no one can support the status quo. So as they say these days, bring it on! Tell me that I am wrong, but then – and here is the rule – also propose a better plan. We have tried everything else, it seems to me, over the past two millennia without any notable success.

It's a man's world and always has been. That is the natural order of things, and man is certainly going to be against any suggestion that women should have more say. So I would expect man to be at the top of the list of those in opposition to this concept. Man has always been regarded as the one in charge. It follows that if he is treated in this way he will always regard himself as the leader; and no one treats man as being more in charge than women themselves. We probably haven't really moved on from the caveman mentality – man dragging his woman by the hair to his cave – although I suspect that the cavewoman was tougher than is made out.

But man need have no fear from anything I am suggesting; I am not advocating equality or empowerment or that women should take over. Let man rule the roost. All I am suggesting is that women in the poorest of the poor societies should be given a tiny fraction of the money that is going around in order for them to start improving their lives. I am not suggesting they should become chairman of the board today. Change along those lines, if it is to happen, will be gradual and natural, and it will certainly not be overnight. In western society we have let women become equal in many public and professional institutions, but those institutions are all designed by men and for men. Women find it much harder to cope in such settings. To take a simple example, in court rooms or conference halls, a man's voice carries far better than a woman's. These places are not usually female-friendly environments by design, so women have an in-built disadvantage even in developed countries. They don't have an easy time, but at least they are part of normal life and part of the workforce, and if they set out to reach the top they can achieve great things; indeed, they can even succeed in developing countries like India, even to the point of leading the country. The difference in the developing world is that ordinary poor women are not seen as part of the paid working population, the natural workforce, working in factories, doing more on a building site than carrying bricks or breaking the rocks for roads. They are capable of much more, but they need the opportunity; even the process of being trained is not poor-women-friendly. Courses should not be so rigid that they do not fit in with the reality of daily lives; nine to five will not necessarily suit all women who have domestic chores to fulfil. This was the main point to emerge from a paper from the EU's Economic and Social Committee: training programmes should be designed to suit the people being trained, not the trainers. It is, of course, different if the woman is being offered paid employment; she will then find ways to make herself available using her extended family and friends to look after her children.

It may come as a surprise to men to know just how much women are doing. This is perfectly illustrated in the DFID report on gender equality and growth, which threw up a number of anomalies. Statistically, in a sample of 96 developing countries women's participation in the formal labour force was low, particularly in the countries of the Middle East, North Africa, South Asia, Latin America and the Caribbean, where in the 20 to 24 age group the range was 37–49 per cent, compared with the average of 55 per cent or higher in other regions. And yet if one takes into account all activity, the report found:

> Women work more than men in almost all regions. The total work of men and women in Peru is such that women spend 15–29 per cent more time in all work activities than do men (Ilahi, 1999). In Africa, 15 of the 17 studies summarized by Brown and Haddad (1997) find women work more than do men. In Nepal, women spend 50–80 per cent more time working than men.[43]

The World Bank in 2006 also found that in a country like Kenya, even though women entrepreneurs make up nearly half of micro, small and medium-sized business owners, and have a good track record in paying off their loans, they have less than 10 per cent of the available credit. The deck is clearly stacked against them, and yet it is not the women alone who suffer as a result: their families could prosper if they had a fairer deal, which in turn would mean their husbands would prosper and then their whole village. The other obstacle to women working, which was noted in Kenya, is that if they go to work in the cities they are often ostracised by their tribes on their return because they had dared to take their 'free labour' away from the village.

Now that the world has slipped into decline, debt and failing economies, it is precisely the time for banks, which have not exactly distinguished themselves when it comes to best practice and probity, to start favouring the more reliable customers and the regular payers. Now that the judgement of our political and financial leaders can rightly be called into question, surely we need to encourage new, female, blood into the corridors of power. If I talk to my woman friends in the civil service in India, for example, they all tell me that they have a much harder time as the men gang up on them. In the UK, what happened to all those so-called Blair's Babes when he came to power? The much-championed female element of his government was gradually whittled away. They left because they were treated so badly in the House

---

43   DFID, *Gender Equality and Growth Evidence and Action*, February 2008.

of Commons, regarded perhaps as mere objects of adornment and not as equals. The Commons is a very male chauvinistic place, worse than a boys' club – it is a bully boys' club. By contrast, the House of Lords used to be an old-fashioned, polite boys' club, which in itself is not something to be derided as they treated women peers as equals.

I suspect men's opposition to this plan amounts to defending their patch. There is resentment against women succeeding. Men even feel somewhat threatened by the mere presence of a female 'high-flyer', and for that matter women are not great sisters when it comes to supporting each other. But this is not about women toppling men from their pedestal: that is man's preoccupation, and he is not under threat from anything I am proposing. Remember, if a woman succeeds in earning a little, everyone around her benefits in the impoverished world I am focusing on; wife and husband will be happy to see their children grow up in a healthy environment and, even better, to be able to enjoy at least a basic education. Who knows where that might lead – from a small Kenyan hut to the White House? Now it seems anything is possible.

I am not actually sure that the church – with a small 'c' – is in opposition to my basic contention that if you give women a little they will achieve great things. But I do fall out with the Catholic Church in particular over its attitude to family planning when it moves from the noble concept of fidelity in marriage to the sinfulness of contraception. The Catholic Church is much more male-dominated than other religions except possibly the Muslim faith. Like all institutions, religions were established by men and everything they do seems to be what suits men. Even when the Protestant faith talks in favour of women priests they only want them to go so far in the hierarchy; the idea of women bishops was enough to cause division, even potential schism. But that row only served to underline the basic point that just as Mammon favours man, so too does God's Church – at least on earth.

The Catholic Church always fights against any kind of liberalisation for women. It is anti-abortion, but does it really believe that it is better for women to die than terminate a pregnancy? I would rather there were no need for abortion, but unless the Catholic Church stops condemning contraception, striking fear into the hearts of its faithful, particularly in countries where the faithful accept everything their priest tells them unquestioningly, you are not going to stamp it out. It is like prostitution and gambling: they have been with us since the dawn of time, and there will always be abortion until we stop having unwanted pregnancies. Remember the statistic – 41 per cent of all pregnancies are unwanted. We owe it to the poor women who can't sustain big families, who live in fear of their men and even sometimes in fear of their God.

So where does it leave women, or indeed all of us? More unwanted mouths to feed and water, and more families to shelter is an attack on us all. Where did this notion of large families come from in the Catholic Church? Is it like the Muslims, who want to populate the world with more followers of Allah? The teachings of the Bible and the Qur'an have been interpreted by scholars down the centuries to mean what men chose them to mean, but I wonder if any god would support an attitude or a faith which is essentially so self-destructive.

Islamic law, *Sharia*, is fundamentally discriminatory against women so there is an inbuilt opposition to this concept: a man is allowed four wives, a woman only one husband; divorce is easy for a man, an obstacle course for women; women, not just wives, are under the legal guardianship of their male relatives; and legally even the lives of women are worth less than men's in cases of murder or injury. No country in the world is immune from the influence of Islam or from what all Muslims believe is their duty, or *dawa*. A tolerant country like Britain may think it has reached a 'working relationship' with the followers of Islam, but it would be a mistake to become complacent. As Patrick Sookhdeo points out in his book on British Islam:

> Some argue that Muslims living in the UK are in a state of *darura* (necessity). According to *Sharia*, extreme necessity transforms the unlawful into the lawful and therefore, by this argument, Muslim minorities in the West can 'live their religions maybe with difficulty but peacefully'. They adapt to Western norms and Western legal systems while voluntarily keeping to *Sharia* norms as much as possible.[44]

Until, that is, they have succeeded in converting the *kuffar*, or infidels. We should remember this when it is suggested that followers of Islam living in Britain should be allowed to be governed by *Sharia* law.

But people are prepared to take just so much before there is a backlash. The Australian Prime Minister, Kevin Rudd, obviously felt he had captured the mood of his people when in a speech which circulated like wildfire across the Internet in March 2009 he told Muslims who want to live under *Sharia* law to get out of Australia:

> Immigrants, not Australians, must adapt. Take or leave it. I am tired of this nation worrying about whether we are offending some individual or their culture … Most Australians believe in God. This is not some Christian, right wing, political push, but a fact, because Christian men and women, on Christian principles, founded this nation … if God offends you, then I suggest you consider another part of the world as your new home, because God is part of our culture.

44 Patrick Sookhdeo. *Faith, Power and Territory: A Handbook of British Islam*, Isaac Publishing, 2008.

The environment is not under threat because we drive cars, fly about in gas-guzzling planes or because the average temperature in British houses is now 18 degrees compared with 12 degrees back in 1970.[45] It is because there are too many of us, and our numbers are growing out of control. The rapidly expanding population is one of the most important threats facing us all, if not the most important, and no one wants to grasp this particular hot chestnut. There are a few lone voices. When Professor Chris Rapley was appointed as the new head of the British Science Museum in 2007 he said: 'My position on population is that I am disturbed that no one will talk about it.' He added that if there were a billion fewer people in 2050, the reduction in carbon emissions would cost 1,000 times less than all the other options.[46]

Nature has a way of sorting imbalances out – often in a violent manner. Just look how the natural order is restored in so many different sectors when life lurches too far in one direction: when nature is threatened and land and forests are destroyed or depleted, rain storms invariably follow, washing away the fragile life, usually of poor people. Plague and disease stalk the land in the same way: Aids is indiscriminate, killing rich and poor alike. An economic system, too, is forced to rebalance; the greed of bankers pushed the system too hard, banks collapsed, and others were forced to think about lending more prudently and investing more cautiously.

Will I find opposition from the politicians? I expect I will certainly find words and conferences and debates, and then what? The notion of focusing all our efforts on women will be dismissed as fanciful, hare-brained or feminist, even all three. The leaders of all the nations who signed up to the MDGs will say they already have placed woman at the centre. But forgive me if I remain sceptical. No political leader – male or female – wants to encourage women ministers. Occasionally some do succeed, even in developing countries, but more often than not those women come from some family dynasty whose name is being preserved rather than being chosen as individuals for their ability – Gandhi, Bhutto, for example. Occasionally it does appear to be on merit: in Liberia, President Ellen Johnson-Sirleaf was inaugurated as Africa's first elected woman head of state. Liberia and Denmark, incidentally, are the only two signatories to the Millennium Development Goals who are actually trying to translate the words of putting women at the centre of the plan into action. President Johnson-Sirleaf is known as the 'Iron Lady' in her country and owes much of her popularity to women voters and the tiny educated elite in Liberia. Interestingly, she herself is a widowed mother of four – multi-tasking to the highest level!

---

45   John Beddington, UK Government's Chief Scientific Adviser, who wrote that most buildings are carbon-hungry and energy-intensive (*Prospect*, January 2009).

46   Charles Clover. 'We need fewer people to halt global warming', *Daily Telegraph*, 24 July 2007.

As I mentioned, we can't expect women politicians to lead on women's issues because it sidelines them from the central work of government. This may come as a surprise, but I firmly believe that without the men being involved, the change I am looking for cannot come about because women will never have enough power to overcome the opposition marshalled against them. For real change to happen in politics or business, it requires the existing power of men.

Perhaps it is a tangential thought when we are facing famine, poverty and economic ruin in many countries, but there will be another significant loss to the fabric of life if we do not find a solution to the economic and environmental problems assaulting us, and it is exemplified in the Indian state of Uttar Pradesh. Here the chief minister, Mayawati Kumari, a female and a Dalit, as I have mentioned, is the embodiment of a potential new attitude in India, but her state is in meltdown. It used to be the cultural heartland of India but its huge and growing population means that most are getting no education and no one has the time to think about culture. It is all a question of survival, and I wonder if it is already too late to effect change in time to preserve its history. It makes me think of a very slow-moving bullock cart lurching along – will it ever change direction, and when?

I suspect that the primary obstacle to this idea, as often with any new idea, will be inertia. Why bother? We have been muddling along like this for so long: how can we change? Why should we change? It is all too difficult. Why take a chance? What is required to make it happen? The impetus must come from the only people who are in a position to make a difference, the business community. Only they have the drive and independence, but will they also be one of the greatest obstacles? It is more than 20 years since the *Wall Street Journal* coined the term 'glass ceiling' to illustrate the barrier women face trying to reach the most senior positions, particularly in industry. In 2005 *The Economist* reported that women accounted for 46.5 per cent of America's workforce and of those less than 8 per cent were top managers, even though historically women held more than half of the masters' degrees being awarded.

The impetus for change, it seems, might be coming from developing countries, according to Pricewaterhouse Coopers who found in 2007 that it was easier for women there to progress to the higher echelons.[47] They surveyed firms in eight countries, ranging from China and India to Germany and Switzerland, and discovered that cultural stereotypes were a bigger obstacle in developed societies. The reason appeared to come down to survival. Samuel DiPiazza, global head of Pricewaterhouse Coopers, said:

---

47   *The Guardian*, October 2007.

In some countries such as Germany and Switzerland, there are cultural and social perceptions of women that make advancement much more challenging. Whereas in the developing world, where there is a huge cry for talent, where there is enormous growth, you must be able to adjust to these norms faster.

The effect of China's one-child policy meant that all children, regardless of gender, had benefited from education and there was no rivalry between siblings for parental recognition which might have favoured a son. Tellingly, Mr DiPiazza noted that some developed countries such as Sweden did treat women more fairly, and he added that there was 'a potential advantage and the developed world has got to pay attention to that'.

The report also highlighted the negative attitude in Germany to working mothers where less than 16 per cent of German women with children under six are in full-time employment, despite having Chancellor Angela Merkel as their head of state. Elisabeth Kelan, the German head of research at the Centre for Women in Business at the London Business School, was quoted as saying: 'In Germany, we have the concept of the raven mother, which suggests they abandon their child if they go to work.' In Norway, by contrast, since the introduction of a quota system the number of women on corporate boards has risen from 6 per cent to 44 per cent. France and Spain have also set targets for women's representation in senior board positions.

I must stress once again that my aim is not to see women running every business or holding most of the seats on a board. I want the effort to be at a local level, and businesses should copy examples where giving women a helping hand does work. In parts of Nigeria women run all the street markets selling food and clothes. It has resulted in a thriving community of women who do have some power. Maybe they were just successful, but the key is that when something works, it grows. When communities and businesses can see what is effective, it will catch on and capture the imagination. We could also draw some lessons from Nigeria on where it does not work. The street markets I am referring to are in the Christian south; in the Muslim north women suffer horrendous abuse and have no such opportunities to show their independence.

As I write this, so much of what we have assumed will always be there is now looking vulnerable. Nothing is secure, from the environment to the economy and even social morality. When opponents to change line up against me, I ask them what is working satisfactorily in any country. Don't just point the finger at the developing nations, even those we might regard as being primitive, but look closer to home. In our desire in the UK to create a comfortable protective society, we have instead gone too far. We have created a nanny state, and a thriving underclass where it is the norm not to work, where large families that we might once have associated with 'backward' societies are now handsomely rewarded with ever larger houses, enjoying benefits for every extra child that is born. Woe betide anyone who speaks up against them because we might be offending their human rights and, of course, it would not be politically correct. What has happened to the notion of parents taking responsibility for their own children?

It is a culture which started in the early anything-goes sixties and, like a virus, it has infected every walk of life. In the seventies, before the Callaghan's Government had to ask the International Monetary Fund for a loan as the pound plummeted, there was so much waste. I worked as a teacher at the time and, having come from India, I was appalled by the waste in the state schools – everything from pencils and books to the fabric of the buildings; there was an attitude that we need not worry because the state would provide and we just had to put in a new order. There was always more where that came from, as it were.

That particular gravy train soon came to a grinding halt. There was 'the winter of discontent', 1978/9, and growing unemployment. There were millions on benefit, and a generation who first could not find work then did not expect ever to work again. Their children, in turn, grew up to realise that they were better off not working and, as we have seen in more recent years, the rest of the world soon discovered that Britain was a land of freebies and handouts. It could not last – it didn't last. Finally, in 2009 a Cabinet minister admitted that Labour had made it too easy for immigrants during their first years in power. 'Initially it was a kind of free-for-all,' Hazel Blears, Communities Secretary, was reported as saying, with 'a lot of people coming as economic migrants, but through the route of asylum seeking.'[48]

But I remain an optimist. In a country like Saudi Arabia, where you would have thought that there is no hope for women, there are the beginnings of hope. King Abdullah, who is probably more tolerant than his predecessors, has made some significant changes. Women are now allowed to stay alone in hotels, checking in alone without a male chaperone. Recently King Abdullah also took a women's delegation with him on an overseas trip, and is even said to want more female ministers. He will undoubtedly face opposition from the religious quarter, but it sounds like progress. If Saudi Arabia can contemplate such changes then there must be hope for us all. The next question is how that change will be made.

It requires conviction and an ability to overcome our natural resistance to change. There is a kind of disbelief and reluctance to try something new, even if we have seen it with our own eyes in the work of countless NGO projects or in a marketplace in Nigeria. If it doesn't work then we are in trouble, because there is nothing else left

---

48 *Daily Mail*, 12 January 2009.

to try. Having seen how much women do, I believe that women carry the world and that they hold up the sky, not just half but three-quarters of it. If I did not feel so strongly about it, I would not be trying to push this solution. In the last 17 years I have been involved with women's issues, which are not the same as feminist issues. I have been to numerous places and seen what women do in their lives – not just projects, but coping with the ordinary burdens of everyday life. If they are given a chance, I believe they will save us all. Women still don't know how much they are capable of. They are doing the work today, but mostly they haven't realised that their work is worth something.

If man is the greatest obstacle to change, whether through his universal fecklessness or his innate desire for dominance, I am proposing that woman comes a close second because she has been brainwashed over generations into thinking of herself as not worth or incapable of achieving anything. The mindset has been so emasculated over generations that women don't believe in themselves. In developing countries the woman sees herself as only there to serve the man and the family, but what man doesn't see is that woman is capable of so much more. If the relationship could become one of partnership rather than of master and slave then both would benefit.

10

FIRST STEPS

As I said at the start, my focus is on the business community. Only the entrepreneurs have sufficient drive and clarity of mind to grasp the enormity of the crisis we face and the scale of the opportunity just waiting to be seized. They alone have the independence to be able to launch the sort of initiative I am advocating without worrying about votes; the only vote they need is the one delivered at the end of the financial year – are we in profit?

Companies need to expand and grow to make money. They are acutely aware that to stand still is to go backwards and, as the UK's Department for International Development concluded in February 2008, gender inequality reduces growth.[49] All the evidence, as I hope I have outlined in these pages, points to massive inequality towards women throughout

---

49   DFID, *Gender Equality and Growth Evidence and Action*, February 2008.

the world but particularly in Africa and the sub-continent. However, I repeat, I am not looking for or even proposing equality here; I am saying that with just a fraction of the opportunities, the aid, the wealth and the jobs already available, women can achieve miracles for themselves, their families and their employers – given the chance. Women need to be part of the paid workforce. Not only are they ready and willing, but they bring none of the failings of gambling, drinking and promiscuousness which their male counterparts have displayed. A woman's loyalty to her work cannot be doubted because her loyalty to her family guarantees that she will never wilfully neglect her children by failing in her work.

Helping women to improve their own lives through work and the self-realisation that they are of value would mean the spin-off benefits would multiply, starting with health. I would like to quote from the Manila-based Asian Development Bank's submission to the UK All Party Parliamentary Group on Population Development and Reproductive Health with its special perspective as an international financial institution promoting development in Asia and the Pacific region. It made three observations:

> First, maternal health is inextricably linked to development, poverty reduction, and social inclusiveness. Maternal morbidity is a cause, and a consequence, of poverty. It reflects unequal access and outcomes for women based on class, caste, wealth and power. Maternal morbidity affects the life and productivity not only of the individual women concerned, but of newborns and other children in the family. Pregnancies that are too early, too often, and too poorly spaced impose significant health, financial, economic and social costs on individuals and households. Maternal morbidity erodes precious human capital. Improvements in maternal morbidity almost always involve much needed strengthening of health systems more broadly. Improvements in maternal morbidity can contribute to social stability.

> Second, despite high levels of economic growth in Asia and the Pacific, rates and numbers of maternal morbidity remain surprisingly high. Four countries in this region are classified as having 'very high' maternal morbidity rates, and a further seven are classified as having 'high' maternal morbidity. High rates mean high absolute numbers in this region. India had virtually twice the number of maternal deaths than the next ranked country, Nigeria …

> Third the level – and the nature – of expenditure is an important factor in explaining poor and inequitable outcomes. South Asia spends just $26 per person per year on health from all sources: lower than Sub Saharan Africa. Per capita government expenditure on health overall in Pakistan is just $9.[50]

---

50   Asian Development Bank's Community of Practice on Health, October 2008.

I am not asking any company to invest directly in the health or welfare of any country. What I am asking them to do is invest in their own business by realising that women represent an untapped asset throughout the world, not just in developing countries, which can help them revive flagging business models or expand successful enterprises. Let the charities and the churches, the governments and the NGOs, continue with their endeavours, but alone they will never solve the problem precisely because they are trying to treat the illness, not prevent it from happening in the first place. My proposition is that for too long now we have being trying to tackle the symptoms, not the cause, of all our problems. Aid workers and no doubt some governments have been struggling with how to help a woman who is sick, how to feed a starving child. Take an organisation like the African Medical and Research Foundation (AMREF), which for more than 50 years has been working in Africa addressing maternal needs from pregnancy right through to the ongoing health of children. AMREF rightly says that Africa needs strengthened health systems, but my contention is that we should tackle the problem much earlier on. If women had the wherewithal to look after themselves properly, including the ability to 'control their own fertility' as the United Nations has called for, then the pressing need for strengthened health systems would not be so pressing. AMREF and all their kind will forever be under pressure, struggling like Sisyphus to overcome unbeatable challenges while women go on having multiple and frequent births. How can countries like Sudan, torn apart by the longest civil war in Africa, ever expect to lower the grim statistic of 2,037 maternal deaths in every 100,000 pregnancies – a statistic which, of course, ignores the life expectancy of the newborn infants, assuming they make it through the minefield of disease, hunger, poverty and probably even war into adulthood?

I am not looking for more charity from business, because charity is not the answer; even if it were a short-term solution, in economic downturns, such as we started to feel in 2008, charitable donations by companies will be the first thing to be cut from the budget. Sally Reynolds, CEO of the charity Social Firms UK,[51] said traditionally businesses improve their image by supporting charities 'but the economic fallout has already seen many companies cut funding for charities and community projects. Worthy causes will suffer but should we blame businesses for putting profits first when facing substantial losses and redundancies?' Absolutely not, and that is why I think the following steps should be taken. While my focus is on Africa and the sub-continent, there is nothing to prevent the same examples and considerations being applied anywhere in the world.

---

51 Social Firms UK aims to create employment opportunities for people severely disadvantaged in the labour market.

Businesses

Step 1 – Evaluate

Just as any business would study a new project, I would ask every chief executive to evaluate his immediate market, and in this case it means his own company. This has to be the starting point. You need to see what you are doing and where women already fit within your existing workforce – if they do at all. As I have said, I am not talking about heads of department: I am talking about the canteen, the laundry, the washrooms and the gardens. Are they male-dominated or led and, if they are, ask yourself why. The reason to put your own business under this sort of scrutiny is to open your eyes to the potential in the community living on your doorstep, working for or supplying your business from the outside. You don't have to go far to start making a difference.

If there is nothing at all within the business then think about setting up something new specifically for women, and from which your company can make a profit. Not only might the initiative help your business but it will at the very least help the local community by giving women that vital start. It might also provide a service or product which local people need. It does not necessarily have to be related to your business, although that is where your expertise lies, and the purpose of this strategy is certainly not to create any new burden – financial or administrative – on your company.

The next stage is to apply the same analysis to your suppliers: are they doing all they could to help themselves by focusing on women as you are doing? I am not suggesting coercion – 'if you don't employ women, we won't work with you' – but leading by example. When they see how much local women are achieving and how their families are benefiting, they will want to copy your approach. A more affluent community quickly becomes a healthier and happier community which will immediately impact the economy of the area and relieve the burden on the aid community.

Step 2 – Scale

The important point always to remember is that I am not talking about a big change of direction for the company; in fact there should be no great change for the business at all, just a retuning. I would advocate something small-scale to enable women to make a little money and for the business to make a profit – big or small. Although there might be aid money available, this initiative should not depend on grants and it is by far the cheapest way to make the biggest difference – any difference. However small the idea you choose to support, it will help, so do it – and that's the point: do it, don't delay, because lives will be wasted while your memos are being exchanged. Even if it does not succeed, virtually nothing in terms of investment will have been wasted.

I recognise that businessmen need to be incentivised to take any action. To put it in plain English, what will they get out of it? My offer is profit – that is my first proposition. Yes, it might be possible to get a grant for building a small workshop or helping a community in some way. But I am not asking for charity, and if your accountants can write the investment off as some tax loss, so much the better. My main purpose is to open corporate eyes to the potential of making money by investing in those who have the least because I know that, regardless of how much money they make, by far the greatest beneficiaries will be the children and the women who for once will be well fed and healthy.

Step 3 – Make it fit

The beauty of this plan is that it suits every business because it can and must be adapted to fit your own business. The concept is the same, but the application is infinitely variable. It is also important to make the project fit the community in which you operate and the women who are available to work. How often have we seen industry sweeping into a town without due regard for local needs, sensibilities or requirements? You must have local support: you have to talk to the village council. In India, Pakistan and Nepal they have the Panchayat system of local government, which literally means an assembly (*yat*) of five (*panch*) people elected and respected by the village. It is essential to talk to them and explain that you are not trying to disturb the order of their lives but are just trying to see whether there are women available to work and why you believe it will benefit everyone – the individuals and their families, the whole of the village community and, yes, your own business. That is the way it has to be sold. If you find it is not beneficial, that is to say not profitable, then you will stop it anyhow. You are asking for their help as a 'partner' in the enterprise, to see what is the best product or service needed. That is what businesses do: they research their market.

There is no guarantee that everyone will welcome your approach, but that will emerge from the initial due diligence, and if the concept is rejected you can look for other villages which are more receptive. Let the people help you decide. India is a democracy, and unless it is illegal they can do what they need to do. In Africa women are working anyway and there is no male control over women in that sense. They may even be producing most of the food for families and looking after their patch of land already.

Step 4 – The cost

The capital investment of this idea is infinitesimal compared with the countless billions already being spent on aid in all its various guises. In most instances it is more a case of refocusing than of finding new money, and at all stages we must remember that this is a profit-generating venture. If it doesn't make money for the company, don't do it. If there is no benefit in kind for the villagers, they won't do it either.

However, if we count the cost of not doing anything at all, it is horrendous. Life will just get worse: the population will go on rising, HIV will spread, deforestation will increase, and hunger and drought will gradually affect us all. If we don't start by doing something at the micro-level of an African or and Indian village then nothing will change.

Why is big business making such a fuss about the Millennium Development Goals when in reality they are not prepared to do anything practical about them? Are they just pretending that they care? What have any of the signatories to the Business Call to Action Declaration actually done? If they think I am being harsh, let them tell me what they have done because I have no way of knowing. How many fewer pregnancies have there been in Africa, how many fewer maternal deaths? If you haven't made a difference, don't you think you should take your name off the list? If you haven't done anything concrete to help, why did you sign up to these goals in the first place? If you have accomplished something then I and the rest of the world would like to hear about your success stories, so others can copy your good example and where they have not succeeded learn from the failures. Initiatives such as cooperatives do work: the Amul dairy launched by the Gujarat Cooperative Milk Marketing Federation (GCMMF) is a good example. It is India's largest food products marketing organisation and provides a good return to the farmers as well as serving its customers. Since its launch in the sixties it has seen its sales rise steadily, and Amul is now a household name.

In Africa the Lake Malawi 'mega-farm' is a shining example of what can be done if we start thinking differently. As reported in the *New Statesman*:

> Investors have leased a huge expanse of land from the Malawian Government to establish something almost unknown in Africa: a commercial 'mega-farm' which, as well as growing peppers for export, produces wheat, rice and maize to feed Africans. It even runs a scheme to feed the old and sick …
>
> When they have grown their crops they send their harvest to the farm where it is processed, stored and sold. The smallholders repay their loans and keep the profits themselves. In the farm's first three years, incomes for 8,000 local smallholder families have risen by up to fourfold. Duncan Parker, who

runs the farm, says: 'We've noticed a real difference in the local economy. Before there was just a bartering system. Now money is changing hands. People dress better. They are making decisions to send their children to school or add a room to their house.'[52]

How attitudes have changed, as the article pointed out, since as recently as 1986 when US President Ronald Reagan's agriculture secretary announced that it was an 'anachronism from a bygone era' to think developing countries could feed themselves. While the project is not specifically women-oriented, it is certain that women are working hard on the farms, but the point is that someone has decided to change the accepted way of doing things.

If it is a question of not knowing where to start, businesses can find out how and where these ideas are operating just by looking at the work already being done by charities and NGOs. Even self-help groups are working; where someone with initiative has started up a project, other women have joined in and they have built a small enterprise virtually without any investment. This must be the common theme: it will only take a small investment to have a huge impact.

But I don't want to be tough on business because only business has the answer. I just don't think they have applied their minds to the problem in the way that I am suggesting. Keep going back to the title of the book: *Woman: Acceptable Exploitation for Profit*. The rewards for everyone are incalculable in terms of profit and social welfare. We all live in one world. You cannot say disease will not spread across the border – just look at the cholera outbreak in Zimbabwe which soon spread into South Africa – and we are spending billions to feed and shelter people. Is it not better for them to feed themselves, to take care of their own health? Is this not the only way for all of us to move forward?

I know there will be resistance to this idea. At a meeting with senior business executives at Unilever House in London in 2008, I tried to encourage them to set up a Parliamentary Group to look into the idea of focusing on women in the way I am suggesting. Most of them said they could not consider doing something only for women – it had to include men. I agreed, but suggested that we should at least start by doing something for women. One of the managers for Africa from Barclays Bank, who was himself African, was the only one who agreed with me that it was extremely important to work with women. No one else spoke up in support of him although they had nothing to say against giving proactive, cost-effective and immediate support for the poorest in our world. There were some mealy mouthed words about there being no role for women, or their business not working like that.

---

52   Mohan Kaul. 'Farming made easy', *New Statesman*, 15 January 2009. Dr Mohan Kaul is Director General of the Commonwealth Business Council.

Why not? They employ people: why not employ women as well as men? My premise is that it is time to start treating women as part of the workforce, just as you treat men. It doesn't matter what the businesses are.

In short, there is everything here that any entrepreneur requires for a successful opportunity: there is quite obviously a market, because Africa and the sub-continent are in dire need of every basic service. Don't think about the boom in India; think about the vast majority who live in abject poverty. There is a cheap and willing workforce: women. They don't need any motivational speeches to work harder; they have a family that needs to be fed. What more motivation does anyone need? And they are a loyal workforce because their priority is not to advance themselves but to support their children. There are no egos involved.

Lastly, there is the opportunity. Never before has the world faced such a combination of financial crisis, disease, hunger, poverty, drought, environmental devastation, and never before has there been such a multitude of mouths needing to be fed and watered. The have-nots will leap at the chance to improve their lives and thank businesses for giving them a chance. It just needs that first step of evaluation which every business can take.

I remind the 60 business leaders of their pledge signed back in 2007, when all agreed that the Millennium Development Goals were not on track. In their Business Call to Action Declaration, they said the time had come 'to live up to the promise' of the eighth Millennium Goal to develop a global partnership for development.

Government

Step 1 – Evaluate

I hold out very little hope that politicians are capable of bringing about the changes I am suggesting, but that is not to say the same principles should not apply. Just as companies need to understand their market, governments should think again about how they are conducting their business; and their business is the welfare of people, not how best they as politicians can cling to power. Corruption is, of course, rife in India, and such a small percentage of what is given in grants or as charity actually finds its way to the people who need it. I am a realist, and I can see that bribery to achieve business deals will continue at every level.

Whether we are talking about New York, USA or New Delhi, India, there is not a city in the world where the principles I am advocating could not be applied with immediate benefit to women. Governments must take a closer look at life under their leadership and ask the question: what more can we do? I know in 2010 there is less money to go round, but this does not require more cash; it requires more enlightened thought, and the scarcity of financial resources makes positive action all the more necessary.

Step 2 – The scale

The business of government is not an isolated affair. If we fail to realise that we are connected by our humanity, we will all fail. We cannot pretend that the 'Dark Continent' is somewhere that nobody goes. Forget about oil wars; we will soon find ourselves fighting over water even in the so-called civilised world. And don't think this is so far-fetched: back in 2004 it was reported that Texas and Mexico were at each other's throats over water from the Rio Grande.[53] The story is a dark omen of things to come. According to a treaty signed in the early part of the 20th century, Mexico is obliged to provide at least 350,000 acre-feet of water annually to the border. But in 2004, downstream of El Paso, the Rio Grande was virtually empty. The combination of a decade-long drought and the demands of the farmers and cities upstream in the US had drained the river virtually dry. The Mexicans were fortunate in having a good supply from a separate tributary, but the Americans invoked the treaty and began demanding their water. Man can live without oil, but not without water. No one is immune. In California they have a vast network of underground water reserves but they are drawing out more than is going back in. Drought and climate change are reducing the snowpack upon which the state depends to fill its reservoirs and the mighty delta. A public education program sponsored by the Association of California Water Agencies warns on their website: 'The current drought in California, coupled with continued population growth and long-term climate change, will make it increasingly difficult to maintain a reliable water supply.'

Step 3 – Make it fit

How long will it take for the penny to drop that there are too many people? Even a small and supposedly wet island like Britain is under threat. In the south-east of England there are also warnings of severe water shortage if the population goes on expanding and we go on building houses at the current rate. The UK is a 'water-poor country' and now near the bottom of the league table for the amount of water we have per head of population.[54] It is not acceptable for people to have large families, and when governments conduct their evaluation, if they have the political courage, they have to question the wisdom of encouraging couples to have more and more children

---

53 *The Independent*, 28 January 2004.

54 ADAS, independent environmental advisory company, BBC 4, June 2005.

by providing unlimited child benefit and other support. Not only are we running out of money but we are running out of space and basic resources like water.

All these are elements of the Millennium Development Goals supported by 189 countries, but we are now over halfway to our target date of 2015, and it was only after everyone had signed up to them that the 'woman element' was added by revisiting some of the terms. Governments, if they are to do anything, should make women the only element of the MDGs for the remaining years – at least then we will have some hope that change will start to come about. It is not just a case of finding a way to increase woman's role; women are just not seen as part of any project, big or small. You go to conferences and women are invisible in male-dominated forums. There has got to be some way of making their voices heard – not to dominate, not to grandstand like hysterical feminists, but just to take note of half the population. You can be a committed feminist in the sense of caring about the lot of women without exhibitionism.

In order to protect women, more needs to be done than changing or adopting legislation to give equal status – in the UK for example such legislation is firmly in place. Rather it is a case of women having the confidence to believe that they can help themselves if they are just given a chance. Governments in developing countries can offer that chance by creating the right environment for businesses to work freely without being seen as some danger to the status quo.

Step 4 – The cost

Without state aid, in a country like the UK, many women would be in great difficulty particularly if they have numerous children by different partners. But who picks up the bill for looking after them? We all do as taxpayers. It does create quite a different picture if you take away the support. It is the state benefits which stop people making an effort to take responsibility; they no longer have the ambition to improve themselves. Why should they if they are getting free handouts and they can still do a few cash-in-hand jobs to make a little extra in the black economy? Why bother to get an education, even when it is all provided absolutely free? These people have no awareness of how the rest of the real poor live. They say they are poor but they don't know the meaning of the word. How would they cope having to walk for miles carrying water on their heads, constantly under threat from murder, rape and kidnap? It puts getting to the shops on the bus that passes by every hour, paying for everything with money you have been given without having to do any work and returning to a centrally heated house you have not had to buy in some perspective.

I am not sure that it would have much impact, but surely mothers with multiple children should be given leaflets so they know what it costs to have so many children and understand the burden it places on society. We have become too timid and too 'PC' to speak up about such things. How many children should the taxpayer have to support for any one woman? And I wonder how much of the child benefit payments actually get spent on the children.

By providing such a safety net, we have created an almost impossible burden on people who work for a living. We have also undermined a basic human desire to overcome difficulty and improve ourselves. The incentive to work has gone out of these people's lives. They will never starve because the state takes care of everything. Without all those benefits, the poorest women could be in almost as bad a condition as the poorest women of the developing countries. But now they have no need to do anything for themselves; there is no upward movement among men or women as there was in the fifties and sixties and seventies, when they moved up into the white-collar jobs or even the middles classes. Today they don't bother because everything is handed to them on a plate. Not only do they not need to work, but they don't want to work. Unless you want to do something, how can you improve yourself? This has created a new category of person that I would describe as being those below the incentive level. And, of course, this handout society is proving attractive to all the parasites of the world claiming alleged hardship and mistreatment in their own countries. I read recently of one woman who was over seven feet tall and was seeking asylum because she was effectively being bullied in Pakistan – she had been enjoying a free council house and £40 a week benefit. Soon we will be taking in the short, the overweight and the excessively thin. I accept that some have a genuine fear that if they take a job they will lose their benefits and if that job doesn't work out for some reason, which might not be their fault, they face a bureaucratic nightmare filling in complicated forms just to get back to where they were. The solution is obvious: the benefits should be frozen for six months, and if they lose their job or have to give it up, the benefits are automatically reinstated. This could give an incentive to try, and it should not be an insurmountable difficulty.

So while I expect nothing in the way of support or initiatives from the governments around the world, including those in developing countries, I at least hope they will not be obstructive towards an idea which has the potential to cut the heavy burden on health and welfare services, such as they are, and in time to generate income. I would also suggest that governments should look again at the Millennium Development Goals and consider, as some countries have done, how they could be better interpreted to suit individual national needs. Just because the target dates cannot be met does not mean the principles should be entirely abandoned, but it is clear that they need to be refined so they fit the reality on the ground and can be implemented sympathetically with local tradition and custom.

Religion

Step 1 – Evaluate

I would use the same four steps for religion, churches and faith groups of all kinds. Some religions are certainly big business and some are effectively rulers just like any government, so they should not be immune from looking closely at what they do and how they do it or being scrutinised themselves.

The issue with many religions is that they have been conceived by men with men in mind. Men are the leaders, the decision makers, the prophets and the messengers of God, and it is rare that women feature anywhere near the upper echelons. Just as with governments, all I would really ask the major faiths is not to be obstructive as they see women standing on their own two feet, gaining confidence and trying to take control of their own lives, particularly their own fertility.

I know this last point is an impossible request for the Muslim faith, some of whose followers can take a harsh line towards women and regard them merely as vehicles to produce children and to serve the men. There are countless examples of mistreatment under the veil of religious belief; in Afghanistan, their treatment was so appalling under the Taliban that women were committing suicide because they could not bear to see their children dying from hunger. They were not allowed to attend school, work, earn money or buy food. Even years after the Taliban lost power, there were attacks on women: two girls were blinded in an acid attack because they had dared to attend school. I know the more moderate-thinking Muslims hold no truck with such people, but in many parts of the world it is the religious zealots that seem to be smothering the majority who want to move ahead.

In places like Saudi Arabia it will have to be the King who shows the way; he could start by saying there will be no more stoning of anybody committing adultery. Why is it that it seems to be women who get stoned – don't men commit adultery? The same goes for honour killings in places like Pakistan – how many men dishonour their family, or are they not capable of it? If Islam says don't treat people like cattle, why do they do so? I can't help feeling it is because it is convenient having all these young girls available to you. It is the feeling that it is man's right; since they can do it, they do it. One newly elected member of the Pakistan assembly told me that we respect our women so much that we don't want them to have a stain on their character – in other words, we kill them rather than let them go on living in some sort of state of sin or shame as they perceive it. But it seems that it is perfectly acceptable for men to be stained from head to toe in the blood of women. It is hard to believe that people can think that they are acting in God's name when four men, again from the Taliban, killed a well-known traditional dancing girl called Shabana in Pakistan's North-West

Frontier Province in January 2009 for behaving in an 'un-Islamic' way and covered her body with copies of her own CD.

I am not trying to rewrite religious doctrine and practice, but I am concerned about behaviour which actively works against at least half of society. I cannot agree with any dogma which encourages multiple and frequent births among very young girls scarcely of childbearing age. There is not a single religious text which says it is right to debilitate young girls, leaving them suffering with fistula for the rest of their days, or a line of scripture which says it is perfectly acceptable for so many hundreds of thousands of young women to die in childbirth. If religious teaching leads directly to more children coming into the world, whose future can only be one of misery, can that be right? What makes it acceptable to blind young schoolgirls with acid?

So when I ask religion to evaluate what it is doing for women, these are some of the questions that I suggest should be asked. I am afraid abstinence does not work in Africa or the sub-continent or anywhere else. We are spending millions on treatment for Aids, but if we could work harder to prevent the disease in the first place then at a stroke millions of dollars as well as millions of lives would be saved. All faith groups should come together to help in this matter by promoting the use of condoms. The Roman Catholic Cardinal Cormac Murphy O'Connor, when Archbishop of Westminster, said give them anti-retroviral drugs instead. So is it better to let them get sick first then give them the medicine?[55] Only 3 per cent of the people get the medicine in developing countries. Words are not good enough – where is the money coming from? The Cardinal said he was advised by African bishops that condoms bred promiscuity in Africa. What does promiscuity mean there? In 2006, Jacob Zuma, the former South African Deputy President, and as of 2008 the President of the ANC (African National Congress), went on trial for allegedly raping an HIV-positive woman. He was eventually acquitted, but was widely criticised when he said that he had showered after sex, believing that this would help prevent him becoming infected. If that is the level of ignorance among the leaders, what hope is there among the rest of the population? A few years earlier, in 2003, President Thabo Mbeki was quoted by the *Washington Post* as saying he didn't know anyone who had died of HIV Aids – this in a country with the largest number of HIV sufferers in the world. I have come to the conclusion that there is no pool of conscience in South Africa; the brutality of apartheid has been replaced with another brutality being perpetrated by African against African.

---

55 BBC, *Andrew Marr Show*, 3 December 2006. Cardinal Murphy O'Connor said: 'I think what I'd like to say to the Prime Minister, it'd be much better if we used that money to provide more anti-retroviral drugs, medicines, for the millions of children and women who are affected.'

Then, in March 2009, Pope Benedict himself dropped what the press called his condom bomb at the start of his African tour en route to Cameroon when he said condoms were not the answer to the continent's Aids problem and in fact 'made matters worse'. His remarks provoked protests from around the world. Alain Fogue, an Aids campaigner in Cameroon, said the Pope's comment went 'totally against all the efforts made by the Cameroonian government and other actors involved in the struggle against Aids in Cameroon'. The criticism spread across Europe. In Berlin, Ulla Schmidt of the health ministry was reported as saying: 'Condoms save lives, as much in Europe as in other continents.' And the French foreign ministry spoke of the 'enormous worry about the consequences' of the Pope's comments.[56] As the protests increased, the Vatican appeared to soften its line, saying the Pope meant condoms 'risked' increasing the incidence of Aids.

Step 2 – The scale

While attendance in church may be falling in many western countries, the importance of religion to many cannot be underestimated and the influence of religious teaching cannot be ignored. It is not just part of politics in some countries, it is politics. We have read a great deal in recent years about the firebrands in the mosques, but what about the influence of religion, particularly among the poor, in parts of the world where Islam is not so dominant?

Le Monde ran an article about the rise of the evangelical churches in fiercely Catholic Brazil and the importance of religion in everyday life:

> In Brazil separation of religion and politics has been part of the republican ideal since the late 19th century. But in real life, the Catholic Church, the evangelical organisations and the leaders of the *kardecist*[57] and Afro-Brazilian spiritualist religions have always influenced politics from places of worship. They have also been party to electoral agreements, with surprising ideological differences, in candidates and parties.[58]

Whether or not Islam, Evangelicalism or Roman Catholicism is on the rise, or becoming the dominant religion, is only important in this respect: are they going to help or hinder? Will Muslims go on believing that it is right for young girls to conceive just because the Prophet Muhammad is said to have married his favourite wife, Aisha, when she was just six and consummated the marriage when she was nine? Will the Pope in Rome go on insisting that it is sinful to use condoms?

---

56 *The Independent*, 19 March 2009.

57 Allan Kardec, whose real name was Léon Hippolyte Rivail (1804-1869), is considered to be the father of spiritualism. He has a large following in Brazil (*Le Monde*).

58 *Le Monde Diplomatique*, April 2005

My purpose is simple, and I would have thought non-controversial: the health and welfare of women. From that, everything I am advocating flows, and that can only be achieved if we start thinking that a woman's life is worth saving, as Dr Mahmoud Fathalla has urged, which leads to Step 3.

Step 3 – Make it fit

Religion by definition is a belief that by following certain rules we can make our imperfect selves better able to meet our maker; some think that may take several lifetimes through re-incarnation; others believe it is achievable in a single lifetime. While I am happy to accept how imperfect we all are, surely one method of improving ourselves is to treat our fellow humans in a better way during this lifetime?

I have no argument with any religion so long as its remit is not actively anti half the human race. What god would be happy with his female follower arriving battered and bruised in his name at the gates of heaven, and with her abuser standing alongside saying 'I have followed the teaching faithfully and my wife has borne many children, suffered intolerable pain in the process until she finally died; so here we stand before you, good and faithful servants'?

If religion does not fit what could only be described as a caring way of life then we have to question its validity, assuming you believe in religion at all. Just as I have urged businesses to look hard at the way they conduct themselves, I think religions, or at least their followers, should do the same, or their beliefs will become irrelevant.

What religion teaches has to make some sense, just as teachers in any classroom have to know what they are saying otherwise it becomes nonsensical. I remember on one trip to Pakistan listening to a doctor giving a lecture to a boys' college – the students were 17 or 18 years old. He was telling them about Aids, but he did not have the words in Urdu to explain himself in a way they would understand. Not once did he say that Aids was a sexually transmitted disease. He could not bring himself to use any of the sexual language because of very puritanical attitudes. After he had finished talking, the headmaster got up and added his advice. He told his pupils to keep away from anyone with Aids and throw them out of the community as though they had leprosy; just have nothing to do with them. He comforted his young audience by saying that they had nothing to fear because they were Muslims and their faith would protect them! The young men were bewildered because, of course, they knew all about Aids. If he had said 'Don't have sex with anyone you don't know, or if you do, use a condom', that would have made more sense to them. Religion must surely have a relevance, and then it can be a force for good.

While my focus is on how business can help society, I do acknowledge the powerful influence of faith; churches and temples and holy places of all denominations can

113

and must use their considerable weight in support of activity which will improve the lives of women, their families and their communities.

Step 4 – The cost

There is no cost to the churches, beyond what they are already doing by providing food for the hungry or shelter for the destitute. Some religions might say the price is too high if it means encouraging the use of condoms or the banning of child marriages, but I can't take on every battle. Suffice it to say that only by example can change for the better come about. When other families see their neighbours prospering because they don't have multiple children, because the mothers are earning a little extra, because there is no disease, then human nature alone will want to make them follow their example. I am not trying to encourage anyone to turn away from their faith, but there is always scope for interpretation of the rules of faith; it has been happening down the centuries as new religious practices spring up and others die away. In the meantime life continues, and my argument is only that women should no longer have to bear the brunt of, frankly, discriminatory teaching.

If the strength of a religion is calculated in terms of rising and falling numbers of worshippers, then look no further than the African missions where attendance is high when a square meal is provided. All I would ask is that those religious schools don't abuse their position of trust by teaching dogma that will only lead to more misery and discrimination. They should accept the fact that the real attraction is not the teaching but the food which is probably helping the children survive.

Media

It would be remiss of me not to talk briefly about the media because their influence probably transcends that of business, government and religion. For many people, all their opinions are formed by what they read in the newspapers or watch on television. For some soap operas are absorbed as though they are an accurate reflection of real life and, sadly, the attitudes portrayed are adopted as gospel instead of an exaggerated and dramatised story.

The media has been dumbed down to such an extent that we are regularly treated to the opinions of Z-list celebrities, sports stars and pop icons. Every one of them has an opinion on global warming but few have the courage to talk about population as being one of the prime causes. One of the voices raised was that of Professor John Beddington, the UK's Chief Scientist, who in March 2009 predicted a 'perfect storm' of food, energy and water shortages by 2030 caused in large part by the growing world population. He told the Sustainable Development UK 2009 Conference that there could be rioting and international migration as the demand grows for essential resources, unless steps are taken now.

If the population had not increased as it has done we would not have global warming. We are exhorted to think about our energy footprint – it is not just one footprint or the energy it is consuming that is the issue but billions and billions of footprints.

11

RISKS AND REWARDS

As we plunged into a global recession in January 2009, it was interesting to read about the 'natural' human reaction to protect our own little corner. When the UK produced its official employment statistics that month, it revealed that the number of women in full-time work fell at nearly twice the rate of that of men – who, of course, outnumber women in the workplace by a considerable margin. The suggestion was that women were being laid off faster than men as bosses tried to protect their businesses from the introduction of longer maternity leave and new flexible working rights for mothers. The press reported that MPs were unhappy that jobs in the 'soft' sectors which are dominated by women, such as catering and retail, were not getting the same government help as the male sectors, such as finance and motor manufacturing.[59] Harriet

---

59   *Daily Mail*, 26 January 2009.

Harman, the Women's Minister, was said to be leading a campaign to shield women from unfair job losses, and the Prime Minister, Gordon Brown, agreed to hold a special session on the impact of the recession on women with the heads of the G20 leading and developing nations when they met in London in April 2009.

I hope such heavyweight attention will have some effect, and I can only applaud the fact that women are receiving increased recognition. You might call it a small victory, possibly even a green shoot to be nurtured in women's efforts to receive equal treatment, but it also highlights how women are still regarded as second-class citizens even in the so-called civilised West.

Fly across the world to Pakistan. In the same month that the above employment statistics came out in the UK, the Taliban in the Swat Valley, Peshawar, were imposing their own interpretation of Islam by blowing up five schools which taught girls. They even invited the local people in one village to come and witness the flogging of women who had dared to think about improving their minds. Having failed in Afghanistan, the Taliban were trying again to impose their regressive doctrine in a troubled region. As the BBC's Mark Urban reported: 'the tribal areas, [moreover] are the key sanctuary for three distinct groups of Islamist fighters: the so-called Pakistan Taliban of Mr Mehsud and his ilk; Afghan Taliban operating against Nato troops across the border; and the foreign fighters of al-Qaeda – Osama bin Laden and his confederates still believed to be hiding in those mountains. If things go badly wrong there, the results could be calamitous.'

They will be calamitous politically but also socially if women get trampled under the religious boot of a misguided interpretation of Islam. News of a deal in February 2009 to bring in *sharia* in return for an end to the insurgency gave me no cause for comfort. One news reporter described it as capitulation by the Pakistan government and warned that the Taliban were unlikely to stop there.

In May 2009 the Pakistan Government seemed to realise the error of their ways and launched a successful counter offensive to reclaim the territory. Sadly this, of course, provoked a wave of indiscriminate bomb attacks by the Taliban in Peshawar and elsewhere in the country.

What I cling to here are the tiny voices of protest which were heard even in the midst of such violence: apparently some dared to speak up in Peshawar to say, very discreetly, that women should be allowed to get an education and train to be doctors and teachers. And if these voices have such courage to speak up in the face of danger then I believe the rest of the world where there is no such threat should follow their example, if not because it is morally right then at least because it is economically wise. The world cannot afford to ignore any green shoot, however fragile, wherever it may appear.

While these two examples are poles apart, they nevertheless in their own way both speak volumes about the way women are regarded in this world. On the one hand, they are disposable and surplus to requirements while the men get on with the serious business of solving probably the biggest financial meltdown in living memory which they themselves have caused. On the other, they are considered inferior to such an extent that education cannot be wasted on them, and so corrupting that they cannot even show their faces in the street for fear of leading man astray by temptation – and if they do show themselves, they should be whipped.

If business leaders are asking what is this to do with them then they should realise that this is their constituency, their marketplace. This is the world in which they are trading, and the people with whom they are doing business. They should remind themselves of the brutal facts of life summarised briefly at the start of this book, facts which cannot be ignored because we are, after all, in this together. We cannot build walls and hope to protect ourselves from the nasty world outside; it failed in Germany when the Berlin Wall was torn down, and in time the wall built by Israel around Gaza will also crumble – they always do. We cannot go on sending food aid to Africa and peacekeepers to war-torn nations – such sticking plasters will not work. We are never going to be immune from disease and violence. They are fighting wars in Africa to gain power because power means control of resources, which means money. They want to be rich: why is anyone surprised that the fighting goes on? We have to find another way. We cannot settle for more of the same.

The global recession should be an incentive to look for new solutions, not just to build a more peaceful and prosperous world – fine ideals for the politicians – but, fundamentally, to help those at the bottom of the heap, in the slums and shanty towns, those trapped on the distant fringes of society. The real glittering prize at the 2009 Oscars was not that *Slumdog Millionaire* swept the board but that a bright light was shining on the extreme poverty in the heart of a major city, even though the featured slum, grim though it was, was far from the worst. I am not aiming high, I am aiming low; by employing mothers we can help children and, as they become educated and mature, the world will begin to recover financially, environmentally, medically and even, dare I say, morally.

I must emphasise that nothing I am proposing is intended to take jobs away from men: the women can do other work. We just have to try to be more creative about finding those jobs. It is very easy to say no – no is one of the shortest words in the English language. But if you try, you might achieve something; if you do nothing, you can absolutely guarantee achieving nothing.

In hard times it is even more important to focus on what can be done that will have an immediate impact at the lowest cost, and clearly the most obvious step is to help control fertility. It is time, in fact well past time, that we came clean and spoke honestly about population growth. What are we scared of – that we might offend someone? Who precisely will be offended? Certainly not the mother forced to bear yet another child, compelled somehow to stretch already overstretched resources to put food in another mouth. Maybe some religious and political leaders will feel aggrieved, but they are not struggling in the slums to survive. How many more conferences do we have to attend on the environment before someone will say 'Let's find a way to help stop women having so many babies'? We can't live in a politically correct world and not say out loud what we are all thinking. This timidity among all our leaders is one of the saddest aspects of today's world. The truth has to be faced if we are to make any progress. Hardly a day goes by without someone making another appeal for a just and honest cause; charities will say give us 60p per day to help a child – but what are they saying? Why is this child in the world in the first place? How many brothers and sisters does it have? How many more 60p donations do you want? Adopt a child and send them aid – how many should we adopt? Fewer children also means more children being educated, which in turn means that you improve the prospects for the next generation. We have to start breaking this cycle of deprivation somewhere, and to me the best way is to have fewer children: only then can children's lives be improved.

The reward of doing something, providing the most modest of jobs or supporting a cooperative, will far outweigh any contributions generous people make to appeals and church collections. At the end of this book I summarise just a few of the initiatives which have been taken and which work; they started as small-scale projects and transformed the lives of many. The snowball effect has been utterly disproportionate to the sums involved. So we all know the concept works: we just have to try it, and this time with the added support of the business community.

What is the alternative? If we do nothing or carry on as before, we will not be leaving much of a legacy for our children and grandchildren to inherit. Do we not owe them more? We can point to amazing technological advances, incredible communications, the ability to defy gravity and fly to distant planets, but why can't we advance in our communications with each other? Why does half the population suppress the other half? How can we honestly say it is a better world? It is not a better world at least for half the population who are raped, stoned, buried alive, hidden away from society, banned from learning. It is not an option to carry on, because we are moving headlong towards disaster – diseases are mutating and spreading, economies are collapsing, entire countries are facing bankruptcy. And why is this happening? Because we are squandering our most precious asset, the asset which has patiently stood alongside man and watched as frankly he has made a mess of things.

How else do we believe that things will change? Will they change because African governments will suddenly stop being corrupt, or because the sub-continent will suddenly stop being corrupt? Of course that won't happen, and some may be surprised to hear that I am not asking for that, because I don't ask for the impossible. I have been a practical person all my life and I see the world as it is. I don't expect man to change, but I do know that everyone likes to make a little money; the reward I am offering mankind, as opposed to womankind, is profit and a realistic and affordable way to recovery. Along the journey, it is inevitable that all our other ills will gradually, and I stress gradually, improve.

As I have made clear, this idea does not require vast investment; but if only business leaders can change their mindset and look again at women as part of the workforce then slowly but surely the prizes will follow. Adding another 50 or 100 women to a mighty global corporation employing possibly hundreds or thousands of people is not going to break them. Two or three women in a small organisation operating in a small town might well make all the difference to that neighbourhood. Just start by putting it into your psyche: ask yourself 'What if I try this? What could possibly be the downside?' People take a long time to work with a new idea, or are hesitant to break the mould, but it doesn't require any talk or debate – just give a straightforward instruction to your HR department: employ ten more women. Just do it first then talk about it afterwards when you come to evaluate the benefit, and in your evaluation consider the benefit to the local community which hopefully will also have prospered and may even have become new customers. In India there are so many successful businesses that it should not be thought of as a western-led idea. In Africa there are also many established businesses – all of them should do something.

Please don't make an excuse of the economic downturn because no big initiatives are going to be started anyway. There is no reason why chairmen and CEOs cannot scrutinise their own businesses to see if they can take women on, which will probably encourage others to follow suit. Some will say there are no statistics, no reports, data or figures to support such an idea. In fact there have been countless studies which point to the neglect of women, the impact on children, poverty, malnutrition. The list goes on, but what have all these reports achieved? Nothing, because they fail to reach the obvious conclusion. There is much wringing of hands, promises to give more aid and support to charities, but charities cannot do any more; they must surely have reached saturation point, overwhelmed by the flood of disasters. NGOs and charities cannot cover the world, governments are not fit to govern, and so it is left to private enterprise. It is only when the world realises that women have value that they will, if allowed, be able to make the enormous contribution they are capable of making and which the whole world so sorely needs.

It does require a philanthropic element because it requires the initial intention to do a good deed. It is the motive behind calling your managers together and asking them to find a role for women. It is a new concept which means having the courage to launch into something uncertain precisely in uncertain times. The motivation has to be to want to bring about fundamental change in society for the good of us all, even if the carrot is only a little extra profit at the end of the year. It is just the starting process to change society, but once that process begins to work there won't even be any need for a spirit of philanthropy. All business has to do is look to regions where women work and the economies are thriving, such as in the Far East.

After all, something convinced those 60 signatories to support the Millennium Development Goals by adding their names to the Business Call to Action. What was their motivation for doing that – the feel good factor, a little PR to be seen to be on message? If I am doing you down then please trumpet all the good works and initiatives that have been carried out so we can all applaud, and more importantly so others can copy and follow your good example. Who has benefited from what you have done since the day you signed? I suspect not very many, but then business is not alone in the stunning but predictable failure to achieve any of the MDGs.

The world's refusal to acknowledge women for what they are and its willingness to accept a catalogue of crime against women in every land, every day, should be a blot on everyone's conscience. My prediction is that if the treatment of women does not improve, if we don't start treating them as equal human beings and if governments don't start implementing the myriad of laws they have already passed then the battle to save the environment, the fight to combat Aids and other diseases and the constant struggle to end poverty and hunger will be lost. Remember the Human Rights Watch world report released as long ago as 2000, which said that domestic violence causes more death and disability among women aged between 15 to 45 years than cancer, malaria, traffic accidents and war, then say we don't have a serious problem. If we can't see women as part of the paid workforce then what position are we giving them?

My hope is that the world will start to treat all people like fellow human beings, and in time women will be able to perceive themselves as having value; the two words I don't use are 'empowerment' and 'equality', because they will come from within when women themselves are ready.

My fear is that my proposition to help the world by employing a few of the most needy women is just too simple an idea. We live in a society where things have to be complex. Unless we wrap a concept up in a bewildering array of philosophy, statistics, analysis and jargon, it cannot be taken seriously. I have listened to so many speeches by highly intellectual Indian women, but you have to decode what they say, and I fear the real meaning is 'Look how clever I am; look at the depth of my thinking and my understanding of world affairs.' In short, they are talking to each other in search of applause and admiration, but after all the words there is no explanation or solution as to how matters could be improved. My message is perfectly straightforward – you cannot crush half the population, mentally and physically, and expect the world to function normally. To put it in male terms: if you don't look after your car one day, it will break down. Well, be in no doubt that the car is about to stall, the engine is misfiring, the petrol gauge is showing empty, you have a puncture and no spare tyre. Neglect and abuse can only lead to failure, and the difficulty today is that the world is broke and can scarcely afford to pay the garage fees.

I would just say this to my critics: don't knock the idea until you have tried it. You have no right to pour scorn on any suggestion if you fail to provide another answer. I know this proposal can work because on tiny, local, individualised levels it is already working, thanks to the imaginative efforts of many charities, volunteers and indeed some businesses. If one woman is healthy and well fed then you can be certain her children are equally fit and nourished, which means there is less strain on whatever health assistance is being provided, less chance of disease being spread, more chance of education. Knowledge leads to confidence in any walk of life: if someone learns how to read, at the very least they will be able to understand the literature warning against the spread of disease.

What I am proposing is not a one-hit wonder, a transient solution like all the economic bubbles which eventually burst when they are pricked by a small dose of reality. This is an eternal bubble. The further you take it, the better the world will become. It can do no harm because it is not an idea founded on anyone else's misery, like the US sub-prime mortgage property illusion. It does not depend on telling a lie, like the packaged and repackaged financial instruments which have crippled our financial systems, and it requires very little investment to make the difference. It does not mean overthrowing any ruler, no matter how despotic, corrupt or brutal, because they will fall in time. Men may say it will mean fewer jobs for them but I see it as quite the reverse, as has been demonstrated in the Far Eastern tiger economies. As local communities prosper and, crucially, businesses see increased profits, there will be more work for everyone, not less. Men in China did not suddenly find themselves unemployed because women became part of the workforce. But even this example is looking too far ahead; I want one firm to try focusing on the poorest women in one town or village and just see the impact. Grameen Bank was dismissed as hopelessly foolhardy and doomed to go bust in a few months; the idea of lending money, any money, regardless of how little, to poor people without collateral was madness. But it took the courage of Mohammed Yunus to take that first step, to leave the sanctuary of academia and meet the real people he found in the village of Jobra near his workplace, Chittagong University. The whole village was in debt and he paid it off with the help of some friends. The money was paid back. He started lending more small sums and, significantly, found that it was the women who were the most diligent about repaying the money. He has now helped seven million people – mostly women. Professor Yunus believed that if all women had access to a loan then they could change the world. But not all women are prepared to take the plunge; they are not all entrepreneurs. It takes a particular sort of person to strike out on their own, but by working together people can build an enterprise, and soon cooperatives spring up.

I am trying to make it easier still by asking the experts, the existing and successful businesses, to find roles for women. They will be queuing at your door when you make your announcement, because women are used to work. They are already working hard but they are not gainfully employed. I want them to work for financial reward, not just as unpaid slaves.

I hope I have convinced at least some of my readers that we have a problem. I hope, too, that a few will agree that there are no other obvious solutions on the horizon to combat the criminal facts of life I listed at the outset. And finally, I hope that just one business leader will have the courage to offer a handful of women some work. Does it really take so much courage to find room for another cleaner or a gardener? I am talking about very small acorns here, very small first steps along the way, because I know what can happen if only we try.

I am not a captain of industry, I don't even have a small business, but if I did I would do the following. I would call all my management and ask how many women we employed, then ask in what capacity they were employed. If I found that we had no women on the payroll, I would find a way of creating just a few of jobs either within my company or with my suppliers. I would not take on the wives of existing employees, because to a certain extent they should already have some support – although I accept that their husbands may not be sharing much of their wages with the family. I would find women who really need the work and focus on helping them. If you are living in a community with 50 per cent black people and you are not employing any of them, you know something is wrong. So look at your community, where half the people are likely to be women, and say yes, in that slum they could do with help, and take on the women, not the men. Sex discrimination and equal opportunity employment laws are a luxury the West can argue about; we are talking of survival among the people at the bottom of the pile. No one gives them a second thought; the mighty business tycoons who fly in and out of India's booming cities never really see the slum dwellers unless a begging child taps on the window of their limousine as they are whisked to and from the airport. As the outside world eyes up the natural resources of Africa, they turn a blind eye to the rampant Aids and the shanty towns. But be in no doubt: in time we will all be affected if we do nothing. You cannot ignore the millions of human beings swarming round Delhi, Mumbai or Cape Town, because one day they will say they cannot take any more; they won't just be knocking on the car windows, they will be tapping at the door of your properties.

My motive for proposing this idea is not out of fear of what others might do, but is based on the realisation that everyone could be a winner. I read the papers full of expert comment about how the economy is in freefall, how the environment is facing destruction, how crime is rampant, how terrorists are already among us, but I see no solutions being offered that are compelling and transcend the boundaries of ideology and culture. We are all together, regardless of race or creed; no single people or faith is going to take over the world; but what we have in common is our humanity. We are men and women living in a single fragile environment. If half the population thinks it can survive by continuously oppressing or even simply ignoring the other half, it will surely fail. While men remain in charge, and that probably won't change, they should use women, not abuse them. It is a very simple solution.

Just try it.

Postscript

Why bother?

What happens to the poorest child in India or Africa matters to every one of us because in some small way that brief, impoverished life impacts on you and me. Everyone knows about the plight of the world: we all know that the Amazon rainforest is being felled at an alarming and dangerous rate – the equivalent of the area of a small country every year; we have been gravely warned about the melting of the polar ice packs and imminent rising of sea levels; and we are well aware that there are millions who lie down to sleep every night hungry. But what should we do about it?

Greener cars and changing light bulbs are just whistling in the dark. We have to be more innovative, and think thoughts which may run the risk of being misunderstood even provoking aggressive, possibly violent, reactions. By now you will have understood that I am convinced that the solution lies with women; not women alone, but men accepting that women are one half of the complete answer – is that really such a difficult idea to grasp? We cannot hope to succeed by ignoring half the population; for the doubting Thomases in the business community who are only moved by numbers, just reflect on the fact that the Fortune 500 companies with women on their boards achieved 53 per cent higher return on equity than those with lower representation.

But follow the thread – women and population are inextricably linked, population and poverty are inextricably linked, and population and the environment are inextricably linked. Instead of that thread becoming a noose which is getting tighter round our necks by the day, I want to turn it into a golden thread of prosperity. Even though population numbers are a key element, I don't start my case advocating enforced reduction in family sizes. This is not some terrifying programme of eugenics, disposing of the weak and unwanted. No, I begin by promoting the health and welfare of women, and to do that I don't want them to be given aid and handouts but a chance to earn some money with pride and dignity. That has to be the starting point, because it is from there that any worthwhile solution will emerge.

You may recall the shocking statistic that 41 per cent of all pregnancies are unwanted – just imagine the impact such a reduction in births would have on the world. Women have to be helped not to have children they do not want, and whatever family planning method achieves that goal let us adopt it, because we really have no other choice. Who are we to decide that one group of people should not be allowed to use contraception because we have some moral scruples? We can indulge in our scruples with our 2.1 children, but let the least well off of humanity, those who will never have the time or even ability to consider the finer points of a moral argument, decide for themselves whether they should have a fifth or sixth child who is likely to be born with a life-threatening disease.

The few lone voices who are speaking up about the threat of a rapidly growing population have to shout more loudly, and those who remain silent should have the courage to support them. This has nothing to do with enforced family sizes: it is about choice, and having that choice begins with women being able to care for themselves by earning a fair wage. This gives them a sense of self-worth; it enables them to care for their existing children and allows them access to whatever family planning solution they choose. In short, it is the only way to give them back control of their own fertility. No one, no religion, no government, no man has the right to say what a woman can and cannot do with her own life, her own body. They will not have to find food for another mouth; they will not have to scavenge for fire wood or sell themselves or their own children into bonded slavery to earn a little money. In fact, this is not anti-Catholic or anti-Pope: it is pro-choice. In an ideal world, a man and a woman would live together in harmony all their lives, bringing up their family which need not be large. Fidelity and mutual respect are all that is required, but until that day dawns nothing should stand in the way of women being allowed to demand the right to care for their own bodies.

Malcolm Potts, Cambridge University-trained biologist and obstetrician from the University of California, Berkeley, has worked on family planning, safe motherhood and HIV prevention in developing countries for most of his professional life. He told a hearing of the UK Parliament on Population and the Millennium Development Goals: 'without realistically easy access to family planning methods and the correct information needed to enable couples – and particularly women – to use them, low income people simply do not have the power to decide whether or when to have a child.'[60]

There need only be one Millennium Development Goal – give each and every woman in Africa and the sub-continent her health and welfare. From that simple starting point everything else follows. The beauty of such a solution is that it does not require billions of dollars of new aid money, and by working through businesses

---

60   Hearing on Population and the Millennium Development Goals in UK Parliament, 11 March 2006.

as I suggest there is no need to get bogged down in the stultifying bureaucracy or rampant corruption of government departments. Indeed, it is only businesses that can make this happen, and I would say that they have both a corporate responsibility and a vested interest in making this tiny commitment to the women of the communities in which they work. I believe both make sound business sense. If you have a thriving and loyal workforce, you will have a productive and reliable business for what will amount to an infinitesimal investment.

Businesses are driven by profits. I am not interested in a philosophical debate about whether they are doing it because it will help the environment and the community or whether they care not a jot about either so long as they make money, if in the final analysis they have succeeded in putting food into the mouths of hundreds of millions of starving people.

Although the aim of this short book is to promote the well-being of the women in Africa and the Asian sub-continent, it is also worth reminding ourselves that the mistreatment of women is not confined to those regions. We could save ourselves billions of dollars if men stopped brutalising women every minute of every day in our so-called advanced societies. We may feel we have come a long way from the days when mothers working in factories had to feed their babies through a hole in the wall, but that humiliation has been replaced with a multitude of other cruelties. All of that can and will change when women are regarded as being of equal value in society.

Where does the fault lie? There is no point in apportioning blame. Everyone can find fault with someone else; we make a ritual of building people up, whether in politics, business, entertainment or even religion, and then setting about trying to destroy them. There certainly has to be change, but I am only asking for a small change. Give a little assistance, and just watch what can be achieved.

If you think about the alternative, you should feel scared: I am terrified for our future generations and our planet. Curiously, the trend globally is for people to have smaller families – with the exception of Africa. In 1970 the worldwide average was 4.5 children per family; today it is 2.6 – so it is not just China that has managed to slow the population growth. Japan, Thailand, Mexico, Morocco, Sri Lanka and Tunisia to name just a few have all succeeded. Most dramatic of all is Iran, where family size has plummeted from six to two – faster than any other country. But there are two uncomfortable facts we must also bear in mind: modern affluent consumers have a much greater impact on the environment than the less fortunate – one American has the same environmental impact as 280 Haitians. But one day the Haitians will be consuming at the same rate as the Americans, and then what happens? The other unhelpful point is that we are living longer, but in our old age we are obviously less productive. In the UK alone it is estimated that the country will need a population of 136 million in 2050 to support the number of non-workers who by then will be living on our tiny island.

But at least the trend towards smaller families offers a glimmer of hope. In the most advanced societies, we are trying by whatever means are at our disposal to reduce the number of children we have. So if we have understood the importance of that for ourselves then surely we can easily see the benefits for those less well off in Africa and the sub-continent. It should then only be a small step to recognise that if we can help women through paid labour to take greater care of their families then in time we would see a reduction in the number of children they have, a decline in disease and consequently more productive communities.

Productivity is the key, and as I write this we face one of the worst economic crises most people can remember. So it is time to ask for everyone's help, and that has to include women.

I would like to end with the story of a young girl who was gang-raped at the age of 14 but whose response seems to sum up everything I have been saying. Her story is one of courage, resilience and the wisdom to recognise that she has to work with all agencies – government, citizens and business – if she is to change the world in which she lives.

Surprisingly Dr Sunitha Krishnan says she was not as upset by the rape as by the reaction of those around her, even family members. She was shocked that people preferred to keep quiet, not only about her attack but about the sexual abuse of millions of other children. But she refused to be a silent victim, and at just 16 decided to devote her life to raising awareness about human trafficking in India where children, boys and girls, as young as three or four years old, are trafficked not just into the sex trade but for their organs and even used in sports where they are made to work as camel jockeys. She wanted to end the silence that allowed such abuse to continue. After getting her doctorate in social work, Dr Krishnan launched her organisation, Prajwala, which means 'an eternal flame', and is now working to raise awareness about the abuse – not only rescuing children but providing them with rehabilitation, mental health and trauma care. In 1995 she opened a boarding school for the children, and her work has spread from Andra Pradesh, where it began, throughout the country. Her campaign has won her awards[61] as well as terrible beatings from those who object to her raids on brothels and sweatshops, one of which left her partially deaf in one ear.

One of the terrible tragedies, and a real indictment of life in the country, is that these children come to regard the trafficking as almost the norm. They become

---

61 Perdita Huston Human Rights Award.

desensitised to the abuse, and develop attachments to the way of life and even to their pimps, and it is common for some of them to leave the safety of Dr Krishnan's hostels and return to the streets.

But crucially for those who stay, the Prajwala does not just provide medical help and sympathy but creates work opportunities. It aims to train the children to earn a living in an astonishingly wide range of activities, from carpentry and print-making to taxi-driving and working in hotels. It must surely be possible for big business at least to match the achievement of one desperate teenager who refused to be pushed quietly into a corner. Dr Sunitha Krishnan lost some hearing after a brutal attack; the question is, how deaf will business be to this appeal for help?

EXAMPLES TO INSPIRE ACTION

- Amul Dairy – initiative started by the Gujarat Cooperative Milk Marketing Federation. It is India's largest food products marketing organisation and provides a good return to the farmers as well as serving its customers.

- ANOKHI – company in Jaipur founded by Faith Singh. It takes in girls and women, and trains them to work in its clothing factory.

- BRAC – development organisation in Bangladesh founded by Fazle Hasan Abed in 1972 to help refugees returning from India. That initial effort has been broadened to tackle long-term sustainable poverty. BRAC employs more than 100,000 people, the majority of whom are women, and has reached 110 million people in almost 70,000 villages.

- Chandraghona Project – Community Health Programme in Chandraghona, Bangladesh, in the Rangamati Hill Tracts. Set up to introduce an income-generating project, it started with a weaving factory providing employment and income for destitute women.

- Goldman Sachs – Lloyd Blankfein, the chairman of Goldman Sachs, launched the Wall Street bank's own private initiative focused exclusively on women in developing countries. In 2008 he announced that the bank would spend $100 million over five years to help 10,000 women to improve their managerial and entrepreneurial education. The focus is to be on practical skills, not theory.

- Grameen – banking system created by Professor Muhammad Yunus to extend credit to the world's poor. Most of the seven million plus beneficiaries to date are women. The first loans issued were for the equivalent of £14.50 to 42 women.

- Lake Malawi Mega-Farm – investors leased land from the Malawian Government to establish a commercial 'mega-farm' which, as well as growing peppers for export, produces wheat, rice and maize to feed Africans. It also runs a scheme to feed the old and sick.

- Plan International – founded in 1937, Plan International is one of the world's largest development organisations. It raises over US$500 million every year to support its work in 49 developing countries, helping children realise their full potential, and includes many programmes for women.

- SEWA – founded by Ela Bhatt in 1972, there are ten SEWA projects in operation in India. SEWA means 'service', but the acronym also stands for Self Employed Women's Association.

- Tata Steel – this private sector company set up an initiative that has seen women trained to become operators and drivers of heavy-duty machinery and vehicles.

EMAIL CONTACT FOR REACTION

I don't expect everyone to agree with everything I say. I don't expect everyone to like what I say. But I would at least expect everyone to agree that we cannot continue as we are with the catalogue of misery being meted out to half the population on a daily basis. Quite apart from being inhumane, it is also, from a purely commercial and practical point of view, wasteful. My suggestion is that, for a tiny investment, businesses can tap into this neglected and abused 'other half' of society and produce profits as well as make an incalculable contribution to the whole of society. I have no doubt that others will have better and bolder ideas; some may even have implemented successful strategies to achieve the same goal. I would like to hear about them, so that their success may be utilised to inspire others to follow their example. To that end, I invite all comments, ideas and stories to be emailed to this address: otherhalf@ whittlespublishing.com.